# SEO BEST PRACTICES
# FOR BEGINNERS

In Copywriting To Generate Traffic To
Your Business Website And Convert
Visitors Into Customers

## Ali Muattar

**ANish Publications**

First Edition: 2019
Second Edition: 2021
Third Edition: 2023
Cover Design: ANish Designs
Publisher: ANish Publications
Printed in the Islamic Republic of Pakistan

Disclaimer:

The information provided in this book is for general informational purposes only. While the author has made every effort to ensure the accuracy and completeness of the information, the author assumes no responsibility for errors, omissions, or inaccuracies. Any reliance you place on such information is strictly at your own risk. The author will not be liable for any loss or damage arising from the use of this book.

Trademarked names, logos, and images mentioned in this book are the property of their respective owners and are used here for identification purposes only.

*To all the business owners who have struggled to attract visitors to their websites, may this book provide you with the knowledge and tools to succeed.*

*Dedicated to beginner copywriters who are just starting their journey in the world of SEO, may this book serve as a guide to help you master the craft.*

*To my family and friends who have supported me throughout the writing process, thank you for your encouragement and inspiration.*

*This book is dedicated to all aspiring entrepreneurs who dream of building a successful online business, may the strategies outlined in these pages help you achieve your goals.*

*To the readers of this book, may you find value in the lessons shared, and may your website traffic and customer conversions soar as a result.*

*The key to successful SEO is to be consistent in your efforts to deliver the best information, education, and entertainment to your customers.*

ALI MUATTAR

# CONTENTS

# FOREWORD

In a modern digital age, having a website is essential for any business looking to succeed in the online marketplace. However, simply having a website is not enough. With so much competition out there, it's crucial to ensure that your website is optimized for search engines and that your content resonates with your target audience.

That's where SEO and copywriting come in. SEO is the practice of optimizing your website and its content to rank higher in search engine results pages (SERPs) while copywriting is the art of creating persuasive and engaging content that drives conversions.

As a digital marketer with over a decade of experience, I've seen firsthand how SEO and copywriting can transform a business's online presence. By implementing best practices for SEO and copywriting, businesses can generate more organic traffic, improve their online visibility, and ultimately, convert more visitors into customers.

In "SEO Best Practices For Beginners: In Copywriting To Generate Traffic To Your Business Website And Convert Visitors Into Customers", the author provides a comprehensive overview of the essential elements of SEO and copywriting. The book covers everything from keyword research and on-page optimization techniques to link-building and social media marketing.

What I appreciate most about this book is its practical approach. The author breaks down complex concepts into easy-to-understand language and provides real-world examples to illustrate key points. The book is also filled with actionable tips and strategies that readers can start implementing right away.

Whether you're a small business owner looking to improve your website's SEO and copywriting, a marketer seeking to enhance your digital marketing skills, or a content creator looking to produce more effective content, this book is an excellent resource that will help you achieve your goals.

I highly recommend "SEO Best Practices For Beginners: In Copywriting To Generate Traffic To Your Business Website And Convert Visitors Into Customers" to anyone looking to improve their website's online visibility and drive more conversions. It's a must-read for anyone serious about succeeding in the digital marketplace.

Saaheer Arman

# INTRODUCTION

SEO is the practice of optimizing your website and its content to rank higher in search engine results pages (SERPs) for relevant keywords and phrases. It's a critical component of digital marketing that can help you generate more organic traffic, improve your online visibility, and ultimately, convert more visitors into customers.

But SEO is not just about keyword stuffing and manipulating search engine algorithms. It's about creating high-quality, relevant, and engaging content that meets the needs of your target audience. It's about understanding how search engines work and how to optimize your website and its content to meet its ranking criteria. And it's about measuring and improving your SEO performance over time.

This book is designed for beginners who are just starting their journey in the world of SEO and copywriting. Whether you're a small business owner, a marketer, or a content creator, this book will provide you with a comprehensive overview of the best practices for optimizing your website for search engines and writing copy that converts visitors into customers.

Throughout the book, you'll learn how to conduct keyword research, optimize your website's structure and content, build high-quality backlinks, and create compelling and persuasive copy that resonates with your target audience. You'll also learn how to measure and improve your website's SEO performance using tools like Google Analytics and Search Console.

So, if you're ready to take your website's SEO and copywriting to the next level, let's dive in and get started!

# PREFACE

In today's digital age, having a website is no longer enough to attract potential customers to your business. With millions of websites online, it's more important than ever to stand out from the crowd and make your website visible to the people who need your products or services. That's where search engine optimization (SEO) comes in.

SEO is the practice of optimizing your website and its content to rank higher in search engine results pages (SERPs) for relevant keywords and phrases. It's a critical component of digital marketing that can help you generate more organic traffic, improve your online visibility, and ultimately, convert more visitors into customers.

This book is designed for beginners who are just starting their journey in the world of SEO and copywriting. Whether you're a small business owner, a marketer, or a content creator, this book will provide you with a comprehensive overview of the best practices for optimizing your website for search engines and writing copy that converts visitors into customers.

Throughout the book, you'll learn:

The fundamentals of SEO and how search engines work

Keyword research and analysis techniques

On-page optimization techniques, including content optimization, meta tags, and website structure

Off-page optimization techniques, including link-building and social media marketing

Copywriting techniques for creating persuasive and engaging content that drives conversions

Strategies for measuring and improving your website's SEO performance

I hope you find this book informative and helpful, and that it inspires you to take action and start optimizing your website for search engines and customers alike.

# CHAPTER 1: THE BASICS OF SEO

Search Engine Optimization (SEO) is the process of optimizing website content to rank higher in search engine results pages (SERPs). Copywriting, on the other hand, refers to the practice of creating compelling and persuasive written content that persuades the reader to take action. In this context, SEO copywriting is the art of writing content that not only appeals to your target audience but also ranks well in search engines.

Search Engine Optimization (SEO) is the practice of optimizing websites and web pages to improve their visibility and ranking on search engine results pages (SERPs). The goal of SEO is to increase organic, non-paid traffic to a website from search engines like Google, Bing, and Yahoo.

By optimizing a website's content, structure, and backlink profile, SEO can improve the relevance and authority of a website, making it more likely to rank higher in search results for relevant queries. SEO is an ever-evolving field, with new strategies and best practices emerging regularly, as search engines update their algorithms and user behavior changes.

SEO best practices for beginners in copywriting are essential because they help you to create content that not only engages your audience but also helps your website rank higher in search engine results pages. Some of the best practices to keep in mind when writing content include:

1. Keyword Research: Conduct keyword research to identify the most relevant and popular keywords related to your topic. Use these keywords strategically throughout your content to optimize for search engines.

2. Title Tag Optimization: Your title tag is the first thing people see in search engine results. Optimize your title tag to include your primary keyword and be compelling enough to attract clicks.

3. Meta Description Optimization: Your meta description provides a summary of what your content is about. Optimize your meta description to include your primary keyword and a compelling call-to-action that encourages clicks.

4. Headings and Subheadings: Use headings and subheadings to break up your content into smaller sections that are easy to read. Use your primary and secondary keywords in your headings and subheadings.

5. Content Quality: Create high-quality, engaging content that provides value to your readers. Aim to write at least 500 words per page.

6. Internal Linking: Use internal linking to connect your content to other relevant pages on your website. This helps search engines understand the structure of your website and the relationships between your pages.

7. External Linking: Link to relevant, high-quality external websites to provide additional context and resources for your readers.

By following these SEO best practices for beginners in copywriting, you can create high-quality content that not only engages your audience but also ranks well in search engine results pages.

# What Are The Seo Best Practices For Beginners In Copywriting?

Search engine optimization (SEO) is essential for any business that wants to increase its online visibility and drive more traffic to its website. Copywriting is the art of creating written content that is engaging, informative, and persuasive. When it comes to SEO copywriting, there are several best practices that beginners should keep in mind:

1. Keyword Research: Conduct keyword research to identify the most relevant and popular keywords related to your topic. Use these keywords strategically throughout your content to optimize for search engines.

2. Title Tag Optimization: Your title tag is the first thing people see in search engine results. Optimize your title tag to include your primary keyword and be compelling enough to attract clicks.

3. Meta Description Optimization: Your meta description provides a summary of what your content is about. Optimize your meta description to include your primary keyword and a compelling call-to-action that encourages clicks.

4. Headings and Subheadings: Use headings and subheadings to break up your content into smaller sections that are easy to read. Use your primary and secondary keywords in your headings and subheadings.

5. Content Quality: Create high-quality, engaging content that provides value to your readers. Aim to write at least 500 words per page.

6. Internal Linking: Use internal linking to connect your

content to other relevant pages on your website. This helps search engines understand the structure of your website and the relationships between your pages.

7. External Linking: Link to relevant, high-quality external websites to provide additional context and resources for your readers.

By following these SEO best practices for beginners in copywriting, you can create content that not only engages your audience but also ranks well in search engine results pages. This can help you to increase your online visibility, attract more traffic to your website, and ultimately, grow your business.

## Why Is The Seo Best Practices For Beginners In Copywriting Essential?

SEO best practices for beginners in copywriting are essential because they help you to create content that is not only engaging and informative but also optimized for search engines. Here are some of the reasons why these best practices are so important:

1. Improve Online Visibility: By optimizing your content for search engines, you increase the chances of your website appearing at the top of search engine results in pages. This, in turn, improves your online visibility and increases the chances of potential customers finding your business.

2. Drive Traffic to Your Website: The higher your website ranks in search engine results, the more traffic you are likely to receive. By following SEO best practices in your copywriting, you can increase the amount of organic traffic that comes to your website.

3. Engage Your Target Audience: SEO best practices are not just about optimizing for search engines but also about creating content that is engaging and informative for your target audience. By creating content that is relevant to your audience and provides value, you can improve engagement and build trust with your customers.

4. Stay Ahead of the Competition: As more businesses move online, the competition for online visibility becomes increasingly intense. By following SEO best practices in your copywriting, you can stay ahead of the competition and ensure that your business remains visible to potential customers.

In summary, SEO best practices for beginners in copywriting are essential because they can help you to improve your online visibility, drive more traffic to your website, engage your target audience, and stay ahead of the competition. By incorporating these best practices into your content creation process, you can ensure that your business remains visible and competitive in today's digital landscape.

# When Can The Seo Best Practices For Beginners In Copywriting Be Utilized?

The SEO Best Practices for Beginners in Copywriting can be utilized at any point when a business wants to improve its online presence and attract more visitors to its website. Here are a few specific scenarios when the book can be helpful:

## Improving Online Performance:

If a business is struggling to attract visitors to its website or convert them into customers, it's important to review its SEO and copywriting strategies. The book can provide practical tips and strategies for improving website performance and achieving business goals.

## Launching A New Product Or Service:

When launching a new product or service, it's essential to create targeted content that not only attracts visitors but also convinces them to take action. The SEO Best Practices for Beginners in Copywriting can help businesses create effective copy that is optimized for both search engines and human readers.

## Redesigning A Website:

If a business is redesigning its website, it's an excellent time to review its SEO and copywriting strategies. The book can help businesses implement best practices for website structure, keyword research, content creation, and link building to improve their online visibility and attract more visitors.

## Starting A New Business:

When starting a new business, it's important to establish a strong online presence from the beginning. The SEO Best Practices for Beginners in Copywriting can help business owners learn the basics of SEO and copywriting to ensure their website is optimized for search engines and designed to convert visitors into customers.

Overall, the SEO Best Practices for Beginners in Copywriting can be utilized in various scenarios to improve a business's online presence, attract more visitors, and convert them into customers.

# Where Are The Seo Best Practices For Beginners In Copywriting Applied?

The SEO Best Practices for Beginners in Copywriting is primarily applied to a business's website and digital marketing efforts. Here are some specific areas where the book's strategies can be applied:

## Content Creation:

The book guides creating high-quality content that is optimized for both search engines and human readers. This includes writing compelling headlines, using effective calls-to-action, and incorporating relevant keywords into the content.

## Keyword Research:

Keyword research is a crucial aspect of SEO, and the book guides how to conduct keyword research to identify the most relevant and valuable keywords for a business's website. This includes using keyword research tools, analyzing competitors, and choosing the right keywords to target.

## Link Building:

Link building is another crucial aspect of SEO, and the book guides how to build high-quality backlinks to a business's website. This includes developing relationships with other websites, creating shareable content, and using social media to promote content.

## Website Structure And Design:

The book guides optimizing a website's structure and design

to improve its search engine ranking and user experience. This includes implementing effective navigation, creating a mobile-friendly design, and optimizing page load speed.

Overall, the SEO Best Practices for Beginners in Copywriting can be applied to various areas of a business's website and digital marketing efforts to improve its search engine ranking, attract more visitors, and convert them into customers.

# Which Type Of Seo Best Practices For Beginners In Copywriting Is Necessary?

There are several types of SEO best practices for beginners in copywriting that are necessary for creating effective and engaging content that is optimized for search engines. Here are some of the most important ones:

1. Keyword Research: Conducting keyword research is essential for identifying the most relevant and effective keywords to target in your content. This involves researching the keywords and phrases that your target audience is searching for and incorporating them into your content naturally and organically.

2. Title Tags and Meta Descriptions: Title tags and meta descriptions are important elements that appear in search engine results on pages. Including relevant keywords in your title tags and meta descriptions can improve their visibility in search engine results and increase the chances of attracting clicks from potential customers.

3. Content Optimization: Optimizing your content for search engines involves using relevant keywords and phrases throughout your content, including in headings, subheadings, and body text. It's important to use these keywords naturally and organically in that provide value to your audience and is not perceived as spammy or manipulative.

4. Link Building: Link building involves acquiring high-quality links from other websites that point to your content. This can improve your website's authority and relevance in search engine results pages and increase the chances of attracting more traffic to your

website.

5. User Experience: Creating a positive user experience is essential for engaging your audience and improving your website's visibility in search engine results. This includes optimizing your website's loading speed, mobile responsiveness, and navigation.

In summary, all of these types of SEO best practices for beginners in copywriting are necessary for creating effective and engaging content that is optimized for search engines. By incorporating these best practices into your content creation process, you can improve your online visibility, attract more traffic to your website, and engage your target audience.

# How Do You Benefit From Seo Best Practices For Beginners In Copywriting?

There are several ways that you can benefit from incorporating SEO best practices for beginners in copywriting into your content creation process. Here are some of the key benefits:

1. Improved Visibility: By optimizing your content for search engines, you can improve its visibility in search engine results pages, which can increase the chances of attracting more traffic to your website.

2. Increased Traffic: By attracting more traffic to your website, you can increase the chances of converting visitors into leads and customers. This can lead to increased sales and revenue for your business.

3. Better User Experience: By creating high-quality, engaging, and optimized content, you can improve the user experience on your website and increase the chances of attracting repeat visitors and referrals.

4. Competitive Advantage: By following SEO best practices for beginners in copywriting, you can gain a competitive advantage over other businesses in your industry that may not be using these best practices.

5. Long-term Results: SEO is an ongoing process, and the benefits of incorporating these best practices into your content creation process can continue to pay off in the long term.

In summary, incorporating SEO best practices for beginners in copywriting into your content creation process can help to improve your online visibility, attract more traffic to your website, improve the user experience, gain a competitive advantage, and achieve long-term results for your business.

## Who Will Use Seo Best Practices For Beginners In Copywriting?

SEO best practices for beginners in copywriting can be used by anyone who is creating written content for the web, including:

1. Content Writers: Content writers who create blog posts, articles, and other types of written content can benefit from incorporating SEO best practices into their writing process.

2. Website Owners: Website owners who create content for their website, including homepage copy, about us pages, and product and service descriptions, can benefit from optimizing their content for search engines.

3. Social Media Managers: Social media managers who create social media posts can benefit from using relevant keywords and hashtags in their posts to increase their visibility and attract more engagement.

4. E-commerce Business Owners: E-commerce business owners who sell products online can benefit from optimizing their product descriptions for search engines to attract more customers and increase sales.

5. Marketing Professionals: Marketing professionals who are responsible for creating and promoting content for their company can benefit from using SEO best practices to improve their content's visibility and attract more leads and customers.

In summary, anyone who is creating written content for the web can benefit from using SEO best practices for beginners in copywriting to improve their online visibility, attract more traffic to their website, and engage their target audience.

# CHAPTER 2:
# INTRODUCTION
# TO SEO

S EO stands for Search Engine Optimization, which is the practice of improving the quantity and quality of traffic to a website from search engines through organic search results. In simpler terms, it is the process of optimizing your website to rank higher in search engine results pages (SERPs) for relevant keywords and phrases.

Search engines like Google, Bing, and Yahoo use complex algorithms to determine the relevance and quality of a website's content to a search query. SEO involves various techniques to optimize a website's content, structure, and backlinks to improve its ranking on SERPs. Some of the common SEO techniques include keyword research and optimization, on-page optimization, technical SEO, link building, and content marketing.

The goal of SEO is to attract high-quality traffic to a website that is likely to convert into customers or take any other desired action. A successful SEO strategy can help businesses increase their online visibility, establish their brand authority, and gain a competitive edge in their industry.

Overview of SEO and copywriting

SEO (Search Engine Optimization) and copywriting are two related but distinct fields that are essential for building a successful online presence. SEO involves optimizing your website and content to rank higher in search engine results pages while copywriting involves creating high-quality, persuasive content that engages and converts your audience.

In the context of online marketing, SEO and copywriting work together to attract more visitors to your website and convert them into customers. Effective SEO requires creating quality content that is relevant to your target audience and optimized for specific keywords and phrases. Copywriting, on the other hand, requires crafting engaging and persuasive content that motivates your visitors to take action.

SEO and copywriting both require a deep understanding of your target audience, including their needs, interests, and pain points. By creating high-quality, valuable content that is optimized for search engines and designed to engage your audience, you can build a strong online presence and attract more visitors to your website.

In summary, SEO and copywriting are two essential components of online marketing that work together to attract more visitors to your website and convert them into customers. By understanding the principles of SEO and copywriting and how they work together, you can create a successful online marketing strategy that drives results for your business.

# Overview Of Seo And Copywriting

SEO (Search Engine Optimization) and copywriting are two essential elements of digital marketing that work hand in hand to help businesses increase their online visibility, attract more traffic, and convert visitors into customers.

SEO is the practice of optimizing a website to rank higher in search engine results pages (SERPs) for specific keywords or phrases while copywriting is the art of creating high-quality, persuasive content that engages and informs the target audience. Together, SEO and copywriting enable businesses to create an effective online presence that drives traffic, leads, and revenue.

## What Is Seo?

SEO, or Search Engine Optimization, is the practice of optimizing a website to improve its visibility and ranking on search engine results pages (SERPs) for relevant search queries. The goal of SEO is to increase the quantity and quality of traffic to a website through organic search results.

Search engines like Google, Bing, and Yahoo use complex algorithms to determine the relevance and authority of a website's content to a user's search query. SEO involves optimizing a website's content, structure, and backlinks to meet these algorithms' criteria and improve its ranking on SERPs.

SEO techniques include keyword research and optimization, on-page optimization, technical SEO, link building, and content marketing. These techniques are aimed at improving the website's relevance, authority, and user experience, making it easier for search engines to crawl and index the website's content.

A successful SEO strategy can help businesses increase their online visibility, attract high-quality traffic, and achieve their marketing goals, such as generating leads, increasing sales, or building brand awareness.

The importance of SEO for website traffic and conversion

SEO (Search Engine Optimization) is critically important for website traffic and conversion because it helps your website rank higher in search engine results pages (SERPs). When your website ranks higher in search results, more people will see it and visit it, resulting in increased website traffic. Here are some of the key ways that SEO can impact website traffic and conversion:

Increased visibility: When your website appears higher in search results, more people will see it and be more likely to click through to your website.

Targeted traffic: By optimizing your website and content for specific keywords and phrases, you can attract more targeted traffic to your website, which is more likely to be interested in your products or services.

Improved user experience: SEO involves optimizing your website's structure and design, which can improve the user experience and make it easier for visitors to find what they are looking for on your website.

Higher trust and credibility: When your website ranks higher in search results, it can help establish your brand as a trusted and credible source of information, which can increase the likelihood of visitors converting into customers.

Better conversion rates: By optimizing your website and content for specific keywords and phrases, you can attract more targeted traffic to your website, which is more likely to convert into customers.

In summary, SEO is critically important for website traffic and conversion because it can help increase visibility, attract targeted traffic, improve the user experience, establish trust and credibility, and improve conversion rates. By optimizing your website and content for search engines, you can build a strong online presence and drive results for your business.

# Understanding Search Engines

Search engines are software applications that index and organize web pages and other online content to help users find relevant information quickly and easily. When a user enters a query or keyword phrase into a search engine, the engine scours its index to identify relevant pages and returns a list of results.

The most popular search engines include Google, Bing, and Yahoo, with Google being the dominant player in the market, accounting for over 90% of global search traffic. To maintain their position and reputation as the go-to search engine for users, search engines rely on a complex set of algorithms and ranking factors to determine which pages are the most relevant and useful for a particular query.

As a website owner or content creator, it's important to understand how search engines work and what factors influence their ranking algorithms. By optimizing your content for search engines, you can increase your chances of appearing at the top of search results and driving more traffic to your website.

Understanding search engines and their ranking factors

Search engines are complex software programs that are designed to crawl and index websites and other online content, and then use algorithms to determine which content is most relevant and useful to users. When a user types a query into a search engine, the search engine uses these algorithms to return a list of relevant results.

Many factors search engines use to determine the relevance and usefulness of the content, and these factors are constantly evolving. Some of the most important ranking factors include:

Content relevance and quality: The content on a website needs to be relevant to the user's search query and of high quality. This means that it should be well-written, informative, and provide value to the user.

User experience: Search engines want to provide users with a positive experience, so they prioritize websites that are easy to navigate, load quickly, and are mobile-friendly.

Backlinks: Backlinks are links from other websites to your website, and they are an important factor in search engine ranking. Search engines view backlinks as a sign of credibility and authority, so websites with more backlinks from high-quality sources are typically ranked higher.

Keywords and phrases: Search engines use keywords and phrases to determine the relevance of a website to a user's search query. Websites that use relevant keywords and phrases in their content and metadata are more likely to rank higher in search results.

Social signals: Social signals, such as likes, shares, and comments on social media platforms, can also impact search engine ranking. Websites that have more social signals are often viewed as more relevant and credible by search engines.

In summary, search engines use a complex set of algorithms and ranking factors to determine which content is most relevant and useful to users. By understanding these factors and optimizing your website and content accordingly, you can improve your chances of ranking higher in search results and attracting more traffic to your website.

## Why Seo And Copywriting Are Important For Your Business Website

SEO and copywriting are important for your business website for several reasons.

SEO helps your website rank higher on search engines, which in turn increases visibility and drives more organic traffic to your website. This is important because the higher your website ranks on search engine results pages, the more likely people are to click on your website and engage with your content.

Copywriting, on the other hand, is important for converting website visitors into customers. It involves writing compelling and persuasive content that convinces people to take action, such as filling out a form, making a purchase, or contacting your business. Good copywriting can help establish your brand voice, build trust with your audience, and differentiate your business from competitors.

In combination, SEO and copywriting can help you create a website that not only attracts visitors but also engages and converts them into customers.

# Importance Of Seo In Copywriting

SEO plays a crucial role in copywriting because it helps to improve the visibility and ranking of the content on search engine results pages (SERPs). Copywriting is the art of writing persuasive and compelling content that aims to engage and persuade the reader to take a specific action, such as buying a product or subscribing to a service.

However, even the best-written copy will not be effective if it cannot be found by the target audience. This is where SEO comes in. By optimizing the copy for search engines, it becomes more discoverable by the target audience, thereby increasing its reach and potential impact.

Incorporating SEO into copywriting involves several key practices, such as keyword research, using relevant and targeted keywords in the copy, optimizing headings and subheadings, and ensuring the content is well-structured and easy to read.

Overall, SEO helps to ensure that copywriting efforts are not wasted by making sure that the content is visible and easily discoverable by the target audience, thereby increasing its effectiveness and helping businesses achieve their marketing goals.

# Benefits Of Seo In Copywriting

The benefits of incorporating SEO into copywriting are numerous and can have a significant impact on the success of your content marketing efforts. Here are some key benefits of using SEO in copywriting:

Increased visibility and reach: SEO helps to improve the ranking of your content on search engine results pages, making it more visible to your target audience. This increased visibility can help to attract more traffic to your website and increase your reach.

Improved user experience: SEO copywriting involves creating content that is well-structured, easy to read, and relevant to the user's search query. By providing high-quality content that meets these criteria, you can improve the user experience and encourage users to engage with your content.

Better targeting: SEO involves keyword research, which helps to identify the search terms and phrases that your target audience is using to find information related to your business. By incorporating these keywords into your copy, you can better target your content to your audience's needs and interests.

Higher conversion rates: By creating high-quality, targeted content that meets the user's needs, you can improve the likelihood of converting visitors into customers or taking other desired actions, such as signing up for a newsletter or following you on social media.

Cost-effective: SEO is a cost-effective marketing strategy, as it involves creating high-quality, targeted content that can continue to drive traffic and leads to your website long after it has been published.

Overall, incorporating SEO into your copywriting efforts can help to improve your online visibility, attract more traffic to your website, and increase the effectiveness of your content marketing efforts.

# CHAPTER 3:
# KEYWORD RESEARCH

Keyword research is the process of identifying the words and phrases that people use when searching for information related to your business or industry. The goal of keyword research is to find the keywords and phrases that are relevant to your business, have a high search volume, and have low competition.

Keyword research is an important component of SEO and content marketing because it helps to ensure that your content is targeting the right audience and is optimized for search engines. By identifying the keywords and phrases that your target audience is using, you can create content that is tailored to their needs and interests.

There are several tools available to help with keyword research, such as Google Keyword Planner, Ahrefs, SEMrush, and Moz Keyword Explorer. These tools can help you identify the search volume, competition level, and other metrics for specific keywords and phrases.

When conducting keyword research, it's important to keep in mind that search queries are not always straightforward and may include variations and long-tail keywords. Long-tail keywords are longer and more specific phrases that often have less search volume but can be more targeted and have higher conversion rates.

Once you have identified the relevant keywords and phrases, you can incorporate them into your content in a way that is natural and optimized for search engines. This can help to improve the visibility and ranking of your content on search engine results pages and attract more traffic to your website.

Keyword research is the process of identifying and analyzing the specific words and phrases that people use when they search for information online. This is a critical step in developing an effective search engine optimization (SEO) strategy, as it allows you to target the keywords and phrases that are most relevant to your business and your target audience.

The goal of keyword research is to identify the keywords and phrases that have high search volumes, low competition, and are most relevant to your business. This helps you to optimize your website and content around these keywords so that you can improve your search engine ranking and attract more traffic to your website.

To conduct keyword research, there are several tools and techniques that you can use, including:

Google Keyword Planner: This is a free tool provided by Google that allows you to research keywords and get information on search volumes, competition, and other key metrics.

Competitor analysis: You can also analyze the keywords and phrases that your competitors are targeting, to gain insights into the keywords that are most relevant to your industry.

Brainstorming: This involves generating a list of potential keywords and phrases that are relevant to your business, and then analyzing them for search volume and competition.

Once you have identified the keywords and phrases that are most relevant to your business, you can use them to optimize your website and content, including your page titles, meta descriptions, headings, and body content. By targeting the right keywords and phrases, you can improve your search engine ranking and attract more traffic to your website.

## What Is Keyword Research?

Keyword research is the process of analyzing and identifying the search terms and phrases that people use when searching for information on search engines such as Google, Bing, or Yahoo. The purpose of keyword research is to understand the language and search behavior of your target audience to optimize your website, content, and marketing campaigns for the most relevant and valuable keywords.

Keyword research helps to ensure that your content is more likely to appear on the first page of search results when people search for specific terms related to your business or industry. By selecting the right keywords, you can increase your visibility, attract more traffic to your website, and improve your chances of ranking higher on search engine results pages (SERPs).

Keyword research involves using various tools and techniques to identify the most relevant and profitable keywords for your business. These may include using tools such as Google Keyword Planner, Ahrefs, SEMrush, or Moz Keyword Explorer, as well as analyzing your competitors' websites, reviewing industry-specific trends and topics, and researching long-tail keywords that may be more specific to your target audience.

Overall, keyword research is a critical component of SEO and content marketing strategy that can help you optimize your website and content to attract the right audience and achieve your marketing goals.

# What Are Keywords And Why Do They Matter?

Keywords are specific words or phrases that people use to search for information online. They are the foundation of search engine optimization (SEO), as they are the words and phrases that you want your website to rank for when people search for information related to your business.

Keywords matter because they are the primary way that people find information online. When someone types a keyword or phrase into a search engine, the search engine looks for websites and content that are relevant to that keyword or phrase and then ranks those websites and content based on their relevance and authority.

By identifying the keywords and phrases that are most relevant to your business, you can optimize your website and content to rank higher in search engine results pages (SERPs). This can help you to attract more traffic to your website, and ultimately, generate more leads and sales for your business.

However, it's important to note that keyword stuffing or using irrelevant keywords in an attempt to manipulate search engine rankings can harm your SEO efforts. It's important to use keywords strategically and organically within your content, in a way that provides value to your readers and meets their search intent.

# How To Perform Keyword Research

Performing keyword research involves several steps, including:

Define your target audience: Before starting your keyword research, you need to have a clear understanding of who your target audience is, what they are interested in, and the language they use to search for information. This will help you identify the most relevant and valuable keywords for your business.

Brainstorm potential keywords: Start by brainstorming a list of potential keywords that are relevant to your business or industry. Include broad keywords, specific keywords, and long-tail keywords that are more specific to your target audience. You can use tools such as Google Suggest or Answer the Public to find ideas.

Use keyword research tools: Use keyword research tools such as Google Keyword Planner, Ahrefs, SEMrush, or Moz Keyword Explorer to identify the search volume, competition level, and other metrics for the keywords on your list. These tools can help you refine your list and identify new keyword opportunities.

Analyze your competitors: Analyze the keywords used by your competitors to rank on search engine results from pages. This can help you identify the gaps and opportunities in your keyword strategy.

Focus on long-tail keywords: Long-tail keywords are longer and more specific phrases that have less competition and can be more targeted to your audience. Identify long-tail keywords that are relevant to your business and incorporate them into your keyword strategy.

Prioritize your keywords: Once you have a list of potential keywords, prioritize them based on their search volume, competition level, relevance, and potential value to your business. Use your prioritized list to guide your content and marketing strategy.

Monitor and adjust your strategy: Keyword research is an ongoing process, so it's important to monitor the performance of your keywords and adjust your strategy as needed to ensure that you're targeting the right audience and achieving your marketing goals.

Overall, performing keyword research is a critical component of SEO and content marketing strategy that can help you attract the right audience and achieve your marketing goals.

# How To Find And Choose The Right Keywords For Your Business

Finding and choosing the right keywords for your business is an essential step in your SEO strategy. Here are some steps you can take to find and choose the right keywords:

Brainstorm: Start by brainstorming a list of relevant topics and phrases that people might use to search for your business or related topics. Think about the questions your potential customers might have, the problems they are trying to solve, and the language they might use to describe your products or services.

Use Keyword Research Tools: There are many keyword research tools available that can help you identify relevant keywords for your business. Some popular tools include Google Keyword Planner, SEMrush, Ahrefs, and Moz Keyword Explorer. These tools can provide you with information about search volume, competition, and related keywords.

Analyze Competitors: Look at the websites and content of your competitors to see what keywords they are using. This can help you identify opportunities to differentiate yourself by targeting keywords that they are not using.

Consider Long-Tail Keywords: Long-tail keywords are longer phrases that are more specific to your business or industry. While they may have a lower search volume, they can often be easier to rank for and can attract more qualified traffic to your site.

Focus on Search Intent: When choosing keywords, it's important to focus on the intent behind the search. What problem is the searcher trying to solve? What information are they looking for? By understanding the intent behind the search, you can choose keywords that are more likely to attract qualified traffic and convert visitors into customers.

Refine and Test: Once you have identified a list of potential keywords, refine your list based on search volume, competition, and relevance to your business. Test different keywords in your content and track your rankings and traffic to see which keywords are most effective in driving traffic and conversions.

## Tools And Techniques For Keyword Research

There are many tools and techniques available for keyword research. Here are some popular options:

Tools for keyword research

There are many tools available for keyword research, including:

Google Keyword Planner: This is a free tool from Google that allows you to see search volume and competition for specific keywords and phrases.

Ahrefs: This is a comprehensive SEO tool that includes a keyword research feature. It provides detailed information on search volume, competition, and keyword difficulty.

SEMrush: This is another comprehensive SEO tool that includes a keyword research feature. It provides detailed information on search volume, competition, and keyword difficulty, as well as related keywords and phrases.

Moz Keyword Explorer: This tool provides insights on keyword difficulty, organic CTR (click-through rate), and priority score. It also allows you to track your keyword rankings over time.

Answer the Public: This tool generates questions and phrases related to a specific keyword, helping you identify long-tail keywords and topics that may be relevant to your audience.

Keyword Tool: This tool generates hundreds of relevant long-tail keywords for any topic.

Google Trends: This tool allows you to see the popularity of a particular keyword over time, as well as related queries and topics.

Ubersuggest: This tool provides keyword ideas and metrics such as search volume, competition, and CPC (cost per click) data.

These tools can help you identify the right keywords and phrases for your business and optimize your content and marketing strategy to attract the right audience and achieve your marketing goals.

Google Keyword Planner: Google Keyword Planner is a free tool that provides keyword ideas and traffic estimates based on search data from Google. It's a great starting point for keyword research and can help you identify relevant keywords for your business.

SEMrush: SEMrush is a popular keyword research tool that provides a wealth of information about keywords, including search volume, competition, and related keywords. It also allows you to analyze the keywords and content of your competitors.

Ahrefs: Ahrefs is another popular keyword research tool that provides detailed information about keywords, including search volume, competition, and keyword difficulty. It also allows you to analyze the backlinks and content of your competitors.

Moz Keyword Explorer: Moz Keyword Explorer provides keyword suggestions based on relevance, search volume, and organic click-through rate. It also provides information about the competition and the difficulty of ranking for a particular keyword.

Google Trends: Google Trends allows you to see how the search volume for a particular keyword has changed over time. This can be useful for identifying seasonal trends and predicting future search volume.

Keyword clustering: Keyword clustering is a technique for organizing related keywords into groups. By organizing your keywords into clusters, you can create more targeted content that addresses the different needs and interests of your audience.

Reverse engineering: Reverse engineering involves analyzing the content and keywords of your competitors to identify opportunities for optimization. By analyzing the keywords and content that are driving traffic to your competitors' sites, you can identify gaps and opportunities to differentiate your content and attract more traffic to your site.

Ultimately, the key to successful keyword research is to use a combination of tools and techniques to identify relevant keywords for your business and to continually refine and test your keyword strategy over time.

# Importance Of Long-Tail Keywords

Long-tail keywords are longer and more specific phrases that are used by people searching for something very specific. They usually consist of three or more words, and they tend to have a lower search volume compared to broader, more general keywords.

Here are some reasons why long-tail keywords are important:

Less competition: Since long-tail keywords are more specific, they tend to have less competition compared to broader keywords. This makes it easier for your content to rank higher on search engine results pages.

More targeted traffic: People who use long-tail keywords in their searches tend to be more specific in their intent and are more likely to convert into customers. This means that using long-tail keywords can attract more targeted traffic to your website.

Higher conversion rates: Long-tail keywords are more likely to attract visitors who are ready to make a purchase or take a specific action. This means that they tend to have higher conversion rates compared to broader keywords.

Improved content relevance: Using long-tail keywords can help you create more relevant and targeted content for your audience. This can help improve user engagement and satisfaction, which can lead to improved search rankings over time.

Overall, using long-tail keywords as part of your SEO strategy can help you attract more targeted traffic to your website, increase conversion rates, and improve the relevance and quality of your content.

# Keyword Placement In Copywriting

Keyword placement in copywriting refers to the strategic placement of keywords and phrases in written content to optimize it for search engines while maintaining its readability and natural flow.

Here are some tips for effective keyword placement in copywriting:

Use the main keyword in the headline: Including the main keyword in the headline can help search engines understand the topic of the content and improve its chances of ranking higher on search engine results pages.

Place keywords in the first paragraph: Including the main keyword or related keywords in the first paragraph can help search engines understand the topic of the content and improve its chances of ranking higher on search engine results pages.

Use keywords in subheadings: Including the main keyword or related keywords in subheadings can help break up the content and make it easier for readers to scan, while also signaling to search engines the important topics covered in the content.

Incorporate keywords naturally throughout the content: Avoid overusing keywords or "keyword stuffing," which can harm the readability and quality of the content. Instead, incorporate keywords and related phrases naturally throughout the content, keeping in mind the target audience and the context of the content.

Use keyword variations: Including variations of the main

keyword or related phrases can help improve the content's relevance and reach a broader audience. For example, if the main keyword is "SEO," variations could include "search engine optimization" or "SEO techniques."

Use keywords in meta tags: Including the main keyword or related keywords in meta tags such as the meta title, meta description, and alt tags can help improve the content's chances of appearing in search engine results pages.

Overall, effective keyword placement in copywriting involves using keywords and related phrases strategically throughout the content while maintaining its readability and natural flow. This can help improve the content's relevance and visibility to search engines and attract more targeted traffic to the website.

# CHAPTER 4: UNDERSTANDING SEARCH ENGINES

How search engines work?
Search engines work by crawling and indexing web pages, analyzing the content of those pages, and then ranking them based on a variety of factors.

When a user types a query into a search engine, the search engine algorithm returns a list of relevant results based on its analysis of web pages. The order of those results is determined by several ranking factors, such as the relevance of the page's content to the search query, the authority and trustworthiness of the page, and the user experience on the page.

Search engines use complex algorithms to determine which pages to display for a given search query, and those algorithms are constantly evolving to provide better search results. Website owners and marketers need to understand how search engines work to optimize their websites for better visibility and rankings.

## Key Ranking Factors For Search Engines

Several key ranking factors search engines use to determine the relevance and authority of a website or webpage, including:

1.      Content quality: The quality and relevance of the content on a webpage are one of the most important ranking factors for search engines.

2.      Backlinks: The number and quality of backlinks pointing to a webpage from other sites is another important factor, as it indicates that other sites view the content as valuable and trustworthy.

3.      Page speed and load times: Search engines consider the speed and performance of a webpage when determining its ranking.

4.      Mobile responsiveness: As mobile usage continues to rise, search engines prioritize websites and pages that are optimized for mobile devices.

5.      User experience: Search engines want to deliver the best possible experience to their users, so they consider factors such as the layout and navigation of a website, as well as the overall user experience.

6.      On-page optimization: This includes elements such as page titles, meta descriptions, header tags, and keyword usage.

7.      Social signals: The popularity and engagement of a website on social media platforms can also have an impact on its search engine ranking.

# How To Conduct Keyword Research

Keyword research is an essential part of SEO and copywriting. It involves identifying the keywords and phrases that your target audience is searching for online and then strategically incorporating those keywords into your website content.

To conduct keyword research, you can use a variety of tools such as Google Keyword Planner, Ahrefs, SEMrush, and Moz Keyword Explorer. These tools allow you to see the search volume and competition level for specific keywords, as well as related keywords and phrases that you may not have considered.

When choosing keywords for your website, it's important to focus on those that are relevant to your business and have a high search volume but low competition. This will increase your chances of ranking well for those keywords and attracting more traffic to your website.

It's also important to keep in mind that keyword research is an ongoing process, as search trends and user behavior can change over time. Therefore, it's a good idea to periodically revisit your keyword strategy and adjust as needed.

# CHAPTER 5: ON-PAGE SEO

On-page SEO refers to the optimization of individual web pages to rank higher in search engine results and earn more relevant traffic. It includes optimizing the content and HTML source code of a page, such as a page title, meta description, header tags, and image alt tags, to make it more appealing to both search engines and users.

On-page SEO also involves improving the website's overall user experience, such as page loading speed, mobile responsiveness, and navigation, to ensure that visitors can easily find the information they need.

On-page SEO refers to the practice of optimizing individual web pages to rank higher and earn more relevant traffic in search engines. It includes various factors that influence the visibility and relevance of a web page to search engines, such as content quality, keyword placement, page structure, and user experience.

Here are some important on-page SEO factors to consider:

Content quality: The content on a web page should be high-quality, informative, and relevant to the target audience. It should also be well-structured with headings, subheadings, and bullet points to make it easy to read and navigate.

Keyword research and placement: Conduct keyword research to identify relevant keywords and phrases to target on each web page. Include these keywords in the page title, meta description, headers, and throughout the content, but avoid overusing them or "stuffing" them in unnaturally.

Page structure: A well-organized page structure can improve the user experience and make it easier for search engines to crawl and index the content. Use descriptive and relevant URLs, include internal links to related content, and optimize images and other media files for search.

User experience: Search engines prioritize pages that offer a positive user experience, so make sure your web pages load quickly, are mobile-friendly, and offer intuitive navigation and clear calls to action.

Social media sharing: Encourage social media sharing of your web pages by including social sharing buttons and optimizing page titles and descriptions to make them more shareable.

By implementing on-page SEO best practices, you can improve the visibility and relevance of your web pages to search engines and attract more targeted traffic to your website.

## On-Page Optimization

On-page optimization refers to the process of optimizing the content and structure of your website to improve its visibility and ranking in search engine results pages (SERPs). It includes a range of factors, such as keyword optimization, content quality, meta tags, URL structure, internal linking, and more. Here are some key elements of on-page optimization:

Keyword optimization: Incorporating relevant keywords into your website content is essential for on-page optimization. However, it's important to avoid keyword stuffing and to focus on the natural and relevant use of keywords throughout your content.

Content quality: High-quality content is essential for on-page optimization. This includes creating unique and relevant content that addresses the needs and interests of your audience. It's also important to use a variety of media, such as images and videos, to engage your audience.

Meta tags: Meta tags, such as title tags and meta descriptions, provide information about the content of your website to search engines and users. Optimizing these tags with relevant keywords and clear descriptions can improve your click-through rate and visibility in search results.

URL structure: Your website's URL structure should be optimized to be clear and descriptive, with relevant keywords included when possible.

Internal linking: Internal linking is the process of linking to other pages on your website within your content. This can improve the user experience and help search engines understand the structure and content of your website.

Mobile optimization: With more and more people accessing the internet on mobile devices, optimizing your website for mobile users is essential. This includes using responsive design, optimizing page speed, and ensuring that your website is easy to navigate on mobile devices.

By focusing on these key elements of on-page optimization, you can improve the visibility and ranking of your website in search results and provide a better user experience for your audience.

## What Is On-Page Seo?

On-page SEO, also known as on-site SEO, refers to the practice of optimizing individual web pages to rank higher in search engine results and attract more relevant traffic to a website. This involves optimizing various on-page elements of a web page, including content, HTML source code, and website architecture, to make it more attractive to both users and search engines.

## Some Common On-Page Seo Tactics Include:

Keyword research and optimization: Conducting keyword research to identify relevant search terms and incorporating them into the content and meta tags of a web page.

Content optimization: Creating high-quality, engaging, and unique content that is optimized for specific target keywords.

Title tags and meta descriptions: Writing compelling and relevant title tags and meta descriptions that accurately describe the content of a web page.

Header tags: Using header tags (H1, H2, H3, etc.) to structure the content and make it easier for both users and search engines to understand.

Internal linking: Linking to other relevant content within the website to help users find more information and improve the website's overall authority.

Image optimization: Optimizing images for search engines by using relevant file names, alt tags, and captions.

URL structure: Creating user-friendly URLs that are easy to read and include relevant keywords.

On-page SEO is an important aspect of any successful SEO strategy because it helps search engines understand the content of a web page and rank it accordingly in search results. By implementing on-page SEO best practices, website owners can improve the relevance and visibility of their web pages to search engines and attract more targeted traffic to their websites.

# Importance Of On-Page Optimization

On-page optimization is essential for improving the visibility and ranking of a website in search engine results in pages. This involves optimizing various elements on the website such as page titles, Meta descriptions, header tags, images, and content to align with the target keywords.

By ensuring that these elements are optimized for the target keywords, search engines can easily understand what the website is about, which improves the website's relevance and credibility, resulting in higher search rankings. Additionally, on-page optimization helps to improve the user experience by making it easier for users to navigate and find relevant information on the website.

On-page SEO is essential for any website that wants to rank well in search engines and attract relevant traffic. Here are some key reasons why on-page SEO is important:

Helps search engines understand the content of a web page: On-page SEO helps search engines understand the content of a web page and its relevance to a user's search query. By optimizing on-page elements like title tags, Meta descriptions, and header tags, website owners can provide clear signals to search engines about the content of their web pages.

Improves user experience: On-page SEO best practices, such as creating high-quality, engaging, and relevant content, optimizing images and media, and using clear and descriptive URLs, can improve the user experience and help visitors find the information they're looking for quickly and easily.

Increases website traffic: By improving the visibility and relevance of web pages in search results, on-page SEO can help drive more targeted traffic to a website. When a website's content is optimized for specific target keywords, it's more likely to rank well in search results for those keywords and attract visitors who are interested in that content.

Enhances website authority: On-page SEO also helps build website authority, which is an important ranking factor in search algorithms. By creating high-quality, relevant content and linking to other relevant content on the website, website owners can improve their website's overall authority and boost its ranking potential in search results.

Provides a foundation for off-page SEO: On-page SEO is the foundation of any successful SEO strategy. Without proper on-page optimization, off-page SEO efforts like link building and social media marketing may not be as effective in driving traffic and improving search rankings.

In summary, on-page SEO is essential for improving the visibility, relevance, and authority of web pages in search results, driving more targeted traffic to a website, and providing a foundation for successful off-page SEO efforts.

## Image Optimization

Image optimization is the process of improving the quality, size, and relevance of images on a web page to improve the user experience and increase the likelihood of the page ranking well in search engine results. Optimizing images involves several factors, including image file size, file format, alt text, and image filename.

Here are some best practices for optimizing images on a web page:

Choose the right file format: JPEG is the best format for photographs, while PNG is best for graphics with transparent backgrounds. GIF is best for simple animations.

Compress images for faster loading: Images should be compressed to reduce file size without compromising quality. This can be done using various image compression tools.

Use descriptive filenames: Use descriptive and relevant filenames that include target keywords to help search engines understand the context of the image.

Use alt text: Alt text provides a description of the image for users who cannot see the image and also helps search engines understand the relevance of the image to the page content.

Use appropriate image sizes: Use appropriately sized images that fit the content and design of the page. This will improve page load times and user experience.

By optimizing images on a web page, website owners can improve the user experience, reduce page load times, and increase the likelihood of the page ranking well in search engine results.

# Internal Linking

Internal linking is the practice of linking to other pages within your website. It is an important aspect of on-page SEO because it helps search engines understand the structure and hierarchy of your website, as well as the relationships between different pages and content.

Here are some best practices for internal linking:

Use descriptive anchor text: Anchor text is the clickable text used to create a hyperlink. Use descriptive and relevant anchor text that accurately reflects the content of the linked page.

Link to relevant content: Link to content that is relevant to the current page and adds value to the user experience. This will also help search engines understand the context and relevance of the content.

Use hierarchical linking: Link to pages that are higher up in the site hierarchy, such as the homepage or category pages, to help search engines understand the importance and relevance of the content.

Use a reasonable number of internal links: Avoid overloading pages with too many internal links, as this can be seen as spammy and may negatively impact user experience.

Use a site-wide navigation menu: Use a consistent site-wide navigation menu to help users and search engines navigate your website and find relevant content.

By using internal linking, website owners can improve the user experience, increase the likelihood of pages being crawled and indexed by search engines, and improve the overall structure and hierarchy of their website.

## Content Optimization

Content optimization is the process of improving the quality, relevance, and usefulness of the content on a web page to improve its visibility and ranking in search engine results. Optimizing content involves several factors, including target keywords, content length, readability, and user engagement.

Here are some best practices for optimizing the content on a web page:

Conduct keyword research: Conduct keyword research to identify relevant target keywords to incorporate into the content.

Use target keywords strategically: Use target keywords in the title, headings, body text, and meta description of the page, but avoid keyword stuffing or overuse.

Create high-quality content: Create high-quality content that provides value to the user and satisfies their search intent. Use subheadings, bullet points, and images to break up the content and improve readability.

Write for the user, not search engines: Focus on writing for the user, providing useful information that meets their needs and interests.

Encourage user engagement: Encourage user engagement by including calls-to-action, social sharing buttons, and other interactive elements.

By optimizing the content on a web page, website owners can improve the relevance and usefulness of their content to users and search engines, leading to improved visibility and ranking in search results, increased user engagement, and higher conversions.

## Best Practices For Optimizing Your Website's Content And Structure

Best practices for optimizing your website's content and structure include:

1.      Use descriptive and unique page titles: Make sure your page titles accurately describe the content on your page and include your target keywords.

2.      Optimize your meta descriptions: Your meta description should be a concise summary of your page's content, including your target keywords.

3.      Use header tags: Header tags (H1, H2, H3, etc.) help organize your content and make it easier for search engines to understand the structure of your page.

4.      Optimize your content for your target keywords: Make sure your target keywords are included in your page's content but avoid overstuffing your content with keywords.

5.      Use alt tags for images: Alt tags help search engines understand what your images are about and can improve your page's accessibility for users with visual impairments.

6.      Improve your website's load time: A fast-loading website is important for both user experience and SEO. Use tools like PageSpeed Insights to identify and fix issues that may be slowing down your website.

7.      Ensure your website is mobile-friendly: With more people accessing the internet on mobile devices, having a mobile-friendly website is essential for SEO. Use tools like Google's Mobile-Friendly Test to check how your website performs on mobile devices.

8.      Provide high-quality and valuable content: Ultimately, providing high-quality and valuable content that meets the needs of your target audience is one of the most important factors for on-page SEO success.

# Writing Effective Meta Descriptions And Title Tags

Writing effective Meta descriptions and title tags is an essential part of on-page optimization for SEO.

Title tags are HTML tags that specify the title of a webpage. They appear as clickable headlines on search engine results pages (SERPs). Writing compelling and relevant title tags that include target keywords can help improve click-through rates (CTR) and drive more traffic to your website. Best practices for writing title tags include keeping them concise (around 50-60 characters), using target keywords towards the front of the tag, and including a unique value proposition or call-to-action if possible.

Meta descriptions are also HTML tags that provide a summary of the content on a webpage. They appear below the title tag in SERPs and can impact CTRs. Writing informative and relevant meta descriptions that include target keywords and a compelling call-to-action can help entice users to click through to your website. Best practices for writing meta descriptions include keeping them concise (around 150-160 characters), using target keywords, and including a unique value proposition or call-to-action if possible.

## Title Tags And Meta Descriptions

Title tags and meta descriptions are important on-page SEO elements that help search engines understand the content of a web page and provide users with relevant information about that page in search results.

A title tag is an HTML element that specifies the title of a web page. It appears in the browser tab and as the clickable headline in search results. A good title tag should be descriptive, relevant to the content of the page, and include the target keyword. Ideally, it should be between 50-60 characters long to ensure that it displays properly in search results.

A meta description is an HTML element that provides a summary of the content on a web page. It appears under the title tag in search results and should provide users with a clear and concise description of what they can expect to find on the page. A good meta description should be no longer than 155-160 characters and should include the target keyword.

Here are some best practices for optimizing title tags and meta descriptions:

Include the target keyword: Incorporating the target keyword into the title tag and meta description can help improve the relevance of the page to search queries.

Write compelling and descriptive copy: The title tag and meta description should accurately reflect the content of the page and entice users to click through to the website.

Keep them concise: Title tags should be between 50-60 characters, and meta descriptions should be no longer than

155-160 characters to ensure that they display properly in search results.

Avoid duplication: Each page on the website should have a unique title tag and meta description to avoid duplication and confusion in search results.

Don't keyword stuff: While it's important to include the target keyword, don't overdo it. Keyword stuffing can result in penalties from search engines and can make the content appear spammy to users.

By optimizing title tags and meta descriptions, website owners can improve the visibility and relevance of their web pages in search results and attract more targeted traffic to their websites.

## Best Practices For Optimizing Page Titles, Meta Descriptions, And Header Tags

Optimizing page titles, meta descriptions, and header tags is essential for improving your website's visibility and ranking in search engine results pages (SERPs). Here are some best practices for optimizing these elements:

Page Titles: Page titles are one of the most important on-page SEO elements. It's essential to include relevant keywords in your page titles but avoid keyword stuffing. Keep your titles concise, informative, and relevant to the content on the page. Limit your titles to 60 characters or less to ensure they are fully displayed in search results.

Meta Descriptions: Meta descriptions provide a summary of the content on your webpage. They should include relevant keywords and a call-to-action (CTA) to encourage users to click through to your website. Keep your meta descriptions concise and informative, limiting them to 160 characters or less.

Header Tags: Header tags (H1, H2, H3, etc.) provide structure to your webpage and make it easier for users and search engines to understand the content on the page. Your H1 tag should be used for the page title, and subsequent header tags should be used to organize content into sections. Incorporate relevant keywords into your header tags, but avoid overusing them.

Other best practices for optimizing these elements include:

Keep them unique for each page on your website.
Ensure they accurately reflect the content on the page.
Avoid using excessive punctuation or capitalization.

Use natural language and avoid stuffing your content with keywords.

Ensure your header tags are used in a logical and meaningful order.

By following these best practices, you can improve the visibility and ranking of your website in search results and provide a better user experience for your audience.

## Header Tags

Header tags, also known as heading tags, are HTML elements used to identify headings and subheadings on a web page. There are six levels of header tags, ranging from H1 to H6, with H1 being the most important and H6 being the least important.

Header tags are important for on-page SEO because they provide structure and hierarchy to the content of a web page, making it easier for search engines to understand the content and relevance to a user's search query. Here are some best practices for optimizing header tags:

Use H1 tags for the main heading: The H1 tag should be used for the main heading of the page, and it should accurately describe the content of the page.

Use H2 tags for subheadings: H2 tags should be used for subheadings, with H3 tags being used for any subsequent subheadings.

Include target keywords: Incorporating target keywords into header tags can help improve the relevance of the page to search queries.

Use descriptive and concise text: Each header tag should be descriptive and concise, providing a clear and concise summary of the content that follows.

Avoid overuse: Header tags should be used sparingly, and should not be used for formatting or cosmetic purposes.

By optimizing header tags, website owners can improve the structure and hierarchy of their content, making it easier for search engines to understand and index the content of the page. This can lead to improved visibility and relevance in search results and can help attract more targeted traffic to the website.

## How To Write Effective Copy That Includes Your Target Keywords

When writing copy that includes your target keywords, it's essential to strike a balance between optimizing for search engines and creating content that is engaging and valuable for your audience. Here are some tips for writing effective copy that includes your target keywords:

Research your keywords: Use keyword research tools to identify relevant keywords that your target audience is searching for. Make a list of these keywords and use them to guide your content creation.

Incorporate keywords naturally: Rather than trying to stuff your content with keywords, focus on incorporating them naturally into your copy. Use synonyms, variations, and related terms to avoid repetition and make your content more readable.

Use keywords in headings and subheadings: Incorporate your target keywords into your headings and subheadings to help search engines understand the structure and organization of your content.

Optimize your meta description: Use your target keywords in your meta description to make it more relevant to the content on the page and increase click-through rates.

Use internal links: Link to other relevant pages on your website using anchor text that includes your target keywords. This helps search engines understand the relationships between your pages and improves the user experience for your audience.

Focus on quality content: While including your target keywords is important for SEO, it's equally important to create high-quality, engaging content that provides value to your audience. Write for your audience first, and optimize for search engines second.

By following these tips, you can create effective copy that includes your target keywords while still providing value to your audience and improving your search engine rankings.

## Using Images, Videos, And Other Multimedia To Enhance Your Content

Using images, videos, and other multimedia is a great way to enhance your content and make it more engaging for your audience. Here are some best practices for incorporating multimedia into your content:

Use high-quality visuals: Make sure the images and videos you use are high-quality and relevant to your content. Avoid using low-resolution or stock images that don't add value to your content.

Optimize images for SEO: Use descriptive file names and alt tags for your images to help search engines understand what your content is about. This can help improve your rankings for relevant search queries.

Use videos to demonstrate concepts: If you're discussing a complex topic, consider using a video to demonstrate the concept. This can help make your content more engaging and easier to understand.

Use multimedia to break up long blocks of text: If you have a lot of text on your page, consider breaking it up with images or videos to make it more visually appealing and easier to read.

Make sure multimedia is accessible: Ensure that any multimedia you use is accessible to all users, including those who are visually or hearing impaired. This may include adding captions or transcripts for videos or providing alt text for images.

Don't overdo it: While multimedia can be a great addition to your content, it's important not to overdo it. Too many images or videos can be distracting and may take away from the main message of your content.

By incorporating high-quality images, videos, and other multimedia into your content, you can make it more engaging and valuable for your audience, while also improving your search engine rankings.

# CHAPTER 6: OFF-PAGE OPTIMIZATION

O ff-page optimization refers to the actions taken outside of your website to improve its visibility and rankings in search engine results pages (SERPs). Here are some important off-page optimization tactics to consider:

Link building: Building high-quality backlinks from authoritative websites is one of the most important off-page optimization tactics. The more high-quality backlinks your website has, the higher it is likely to rank in search engine results.

Social media marketing: Social media can be a powerful tool for promoting your website and building your online presence. By regularly posting and engaging with your followers on social media, you can drive more traffic to your website and improve your visibility in search engine results.

Guest blogging: Writing high-quality guest posts for other websites in your industry can help you build your online reputation and attract new visitors to your website.

Influencer marketing: Partnering with influencers or industry experts can help you reach a wider audience and build credibility for your brand.

Online directories: Listing your business in online directories can help improve your visibility in search engine results and drive more traffic to your website.

Brand mentions: Building brand mentions on other websites or social media platforms can help increase your brand awareness and improve your search engine rankings.

Overall, off-page optimization is an important part of any SEO strategy. By focusing on high-quality link building, social media marketing, guest blogging, and other tactics, you can improve your website's visibility, attract more traffic, and ultimately drive more conversions.

## What Is Off-Page Seo?

Off-page SEO refers to the optimization techniques and strategies used to improve the visibility and ranking of a website on search engine results pages (SERPs) through activities that take place outside of the website itself.

While on-page SEO refers to optimizing the content and HTML source code of a website, off-page SEO involves actions such as building backlinks, social media marketing, influencer outreach, and online reputation management. Off-page SEO aims to demonstrate the popularity, relevance, and authority of a website to search engines and users.

Some of the most important off-page SEO factors include:

Backlinks: Backlinks are links from other websites that point to your website. The quality and quantity of backlinks are important ranking factors, as they indicate that other websites view your content as valuable and trustworthy.

Social media: Social media platforms are a great way to promote your website, engage with your audience, and increase your online visibility.

Online reputation management: Online reputation management involves monitoring and managing your brand's reputation online, including addressing negative reviews or comments, and managing your online presence on third-party websites.

Influencer outreach: Influencer marketing is a popular off-page SEO technique that involves partnering with influential individuals or organizations to promote your brand or products.

Local SEO: Local SEO involves optimizing your website and online presence for local search results. This includes optimizing your Google My Business listing, building local citations, and generating positive local reviews.

Overall, off-page SEO is an essential part of any successful search engine optimization strategy, as it helps to demonstrate the popularity, relevance, and authority of a website to search engines and users, and can significantly improve a website's visibility and ranking in search results.

## Off-Page Seo

Off-page SEO refers to the optimization activities that are performed outside of your website to improve its ranking in search engines. Unlike on-page SEO, which focuses on improving your website's content and structure, off-page SEO deals with building the reputation and authority of your website in the online community. This is achieved through various techniques such as link building, social media marketing, and influencer outreach.

The goal of off-page SEO is to improve your website's visibility, credibility, and reputation in the eyes of search engines, as well as potential customers. By building a strong online presence through off-page optimization techniques, you can attract more traffic to your website, generate more leads, and ultimately increase your revenue.

Some of the key off-page optimization strategies include building high-quality backlinks to your website, establishing a strong social media presence, engaging with your audience on forums and other online communities, and collaborating with influencers and other industry experts.

Off-page SEO refers to the actions taken outside of your website to improve its ranking and visibility in search engine results. Off-page SEO includes factors such as backlinks, social media marketing, and online reputation management.

Here are some of the key elements of off-page SEO:

Backlinks: Backlinks are links from other websites to your website. They are an important ranking factor for search engines, as they indicate that other sites view your content as valuable and trustworthy. Building high-quality backlinks from reputable websites is an essential part of off-page SEO.

Social media marketing: Social media marketing involves promoting your website and content on social media platforms such as Facebook, Twitter, LinkedIn, and Instagram. By engaging with your target audience on social media, you can increase brand awareness and drive traffic to your website.

Online reputation management: Online reputation management involves monitoring and managing your online presence and reputation. By responding to customer feedback and addressing negative reviews and comments, you can improve your reputation and credibility in the eyes of search engines and potential customers.

Influencer marketing: Influencer marketing involves partnering with influential individuals or organizations to promote your brand or products. By leveraging the reach and influence of others in your industry or niche, you can increase brand awareness and drive traffic to your website.

By focusing on off-page SEO, website owners can improve the visibility and credibility of their website, increase brand awareness, and drive targeted traffic to their site. However, it's important to note that off-page SEO requires ongoing effort and investment to be effective.

# The Role Of Backlinks In Seo

Backlinks are links that point from one website to another. In SEO, backlinks are important because they are considered by search engines as a signal of the website's popularity and authority. The more high-quality backlinks a website has, the more likely it is to rank higher in search engine results pages (SERPs).

Backlinks are considered a vote of confidence from other websites. When a website links to another website, it is essentially endorsing the content on that website. Search engines view this endorsement as a positive signal and use it as a ranking factor.

However, not all backlinks are created equal. Search engines also consider the quality and relevance of the linking website when evaluating the backlink. A backlink from a high-authority website in your industry is considered more valuable than a backlink from a low-authority or unrelated website.

It's important to note that not all backlinks are created equal. Search engines also consider the quality and relevance of the linking website when evaluating the backlink. A backlink from a high-authority website in your industry is considered more valuable than a backlink from a low-authority or unrelated website.

Overall, backlinks play a crucial role in SEO by helping to establish a website's authority and improve its visibility in search engine results pages. As a result, building high-quality backlinks from relevant and authoritative websites should be a key part of any SEO strategy.

The role of backlinks in SEO

Backlinks play a crucial role in off-page SEO. They are links from other websites that lead to your website. The number and quality of backlinks to your website are among the most important factors that search engines use to determine your website's ranking in search results. High-quality backlinks from authoritative websites can improve your website's credibility and authority, leading to higher search engine rankings and more traffic. However, low-quality or spammy backlinks can hurt your website's ranking and reputation. It is essential to focus on building high-quality backlinks through ethical and effective techniques such as guest blogging, broken link building, and social media outreach.

## Importance Of Off-Page Seo

Off-page SEO is important because it helps to improve the visibility and ranking of a website on search engine results pages (SERPs) through activities that take place outside of the website itself. Here are some of the key reasons why off-page SEO is important:

Improved search engine ranking: Backlinks from other high-quality websites are a key ranking factor for search engines. By building high-quality backlinks from reputable websites, you can improve the ranking of your website on SERPs.

Increased traffic: Off-page SEO can help to drive traffic to your website from sources other than search engines, such as social media, referral traffic from backlinks, and influencer marketing.

Enhanced brand reputation: Off-page SEO can help to build your brand's reputation and credibility by demonstrating your expertise, authority, and trustworthiness in your industry or niche.

Greater online visibility: By promoting your website and content through social media, influencer marketing, and other off-page SEO strategies, you can increase your online visibility and reach a wider audience.

Competitive advantage: By investing in off-page SEO, you can gain a competitive advantage over other websites in your industry or niche, as you will be more visible and authoritative in the eyes of search engines and users.

Overall, off-page SEO is an essential part of any successful search engine optimization strategy, as it helps to demonstrate the popularity, relevance, and authority of a website to search engines and users, and can significantly improve a website's visibility, ranking, and traffic.

Back linking

Back linking refers to the process of obtaining links from other websites that point to your website. Backlinks are a key off-page SEO factor that search engines use to determine the popularity, relevance, and authority of a website.

Backlinks are important because they signal to search engines that other websites view your content as valuable and trustworthy. When a high-quality website links to your website, it indicates to search engines that your content is relevant and authoritative in your industry or niche, which can help to improve your website's ranking on search engine results pages (SERPs).

However, it's important to note that not all backlinks are created equal. Search engines place a greater emphasis on the quality and relevance of backlinks, rather than just the quantity. Backlinks from authoritative websites that are relevant to your industry or niche are more valuable than low-quality backlinks from spammy or unrelated websites.

There are many strategies for building high-quality backlinks, including guest blogging, broken link building, and influencer outreach. However, it's important to approach backlinking with a long-term mindset and focus on building a natural and diverse backlink profile, rather than relying on spammy or black hat techniques that can lead to penalties from search engines.

# Guest Blogging

Guest blogging, also known as guest posting, is the practice of writing and publishing an article or blog post on another website or blog to build backlinks, drive traffic to your website, and increase your online presence.

Guest blogging can be an effective strategy for building backlinks to your website, as each guest post typically includes a link back to your website or blog. Backlinks are an important factor in search engine optimization (SEO), as they signal to search engines that your website is reputable and authoritative. By guest blogging on high-quality, relevant websites, you can build a strong backlink profile and improve your search engine rankings.

In addition to building backlinks, guest blogging can also help to increase your online presence and drive traffic to your website. By writing high-quality, informative blog posts that are relevant to your target audience, you can attract new visitors to your website and establish yourself as an authority in your industry or niche.

To get started with guest blogging, you can identify high-quality, relevant websites that accept guest posts in your industry or niche. You can then reach out to these websites with a pitch for a guest post, or respond to their guest blogging guidelines. When writing your guest post, be sure to provide high-quality, informative content that is relevant to the website's audience, and include a link back to your website or blog in your author bio.

# How To Avoid Black Hat Seo Tactics

Black hat SEO tactics are techniques that violate search engine guidelines in an attempt to manipulate search engine rankings. These tactics are typically seen as unethical and can result in penalties or even a complete ban from search engines.

Here are some tips to help you avoid black hat SEO tactics:

1.      Focus on creating high-quality content that is relevant and valuable to your audience.

2.      Avoid using hidden text or links, which are designed to manipulate search engine rankings.

3.      Don't stuff your content with keywords, as this can make it difficult for users to read and can result in penalties from search engines.

4.      Don't participate in link schemes, which involve buying or trading links in an attempt to improve search engine rankings.

5.      Avoid creating duplicate content, as this can confuse search engines and result in lower rankings.

By following ethical SEO practices and focusing on creating high-quality content, you can improve your search engine rankings without risking penalties or a ban from search engines.

## Influencer Marketing

Influencer marketing is a type of marketing that involves partnering with individuals who have a large following on social media platforms to promote a product, service, or brand. These individuals, known as influencers, can reach a large and engaged audience on social media and can be effective in driving engagement, brand awareness, and sales.

Influencer marketing typically involves identifying relevant influencers who have a large following in your target audience and partnering with them to create content or promote your brand. This can involve paying the influencer directly, providing them with free products or services, or offering them an affiliate commission on any sales generated through their promotion.

Influencer marketing can be effective for several reasons. First, influencers have built a loyal following of engaged followers who trust their recommendations and opinions. By partnering with an influencer, you can tap into this trust and leverage it to promote your brand or product.

In addition, influencer marketing can be a cost-effective way to reach a large audience on social media. By partnering with an influencer, you can potentially reach thousands or even millions of people with a single post, without having to invest heavily in advertising or other marketing efforts.

However, it's important to note that influencer marketing is not a one-size-fits-all approach, and success will depend on finding the right influencers who are a good fit for your brand and target audience. It's also important to ensure that any influencer partnerships are authentic and transparent and comply with all relevant advertising and disclosure guidelines.

## Social Media And Its Impact On Seo

Social media can indirectly impact SEO by increasing brand visibility, driving website traffic, and building high-quality backlinks. When your content is shared on social media, it can increase your reach and attract more visitors to your website. This increased traffic can also signal to search engines that your content is relevant and valuable, potentially boosting your search engine rankings.

Additionally, social media profiles themselves can rank in search engine results pages (SERPs). By optimizing your social media profiles with relevant keywords and linking back to your website, you can increase the chances of your profiles appearing in search results and driving traffic to your site.

Finally, social media can be a powerful tool for building relationships with other websites and influencers in your industry. By engaging with these individuals and sharing their content, you can increase the chances of them linking back to your site, which can further boost your search engine rankings.

## Social Media Marketing

Social media marketing is the process of using social media platforms to promote a product or service, build brand awareness, engage with customers, and drive website traffic. Social media marketing involves creating and sharing content, as well as engaging with followers and other users on social media platforms such as Facebook, Twitter, Instagram, LinkedIn, and YouTube.

Social media marketing is important because it can help businesses to:

Increase brand awareness: Social media platforms offer a highly effective way to reach a large and diverse audience and build brand recognition and awareness.

Improve customer engagement: Social media platforms provide a direct and immediate way to interact with customers and respond to their questions, comments, and feedback.

Drive website traffic: By sharing content and links to your website on social media platforms, you can drive traffic to your website and increase your search engine ranking.

Generate leads and sales: Social media platforms can be used to promote products and services, offer special promotions and discounts, and drive sales and leads.

Build customer loyalty: By providing valuable content, engaging with customers, and building a strong social media presence, businesses can build a loyal following and strengthen customer relationships.

Overall, social media marketing is an essential part of any comprehensive marketing strategy, and can be highly effective in reaching and engaging with a target audience, building brand awareness, and driving website traffic and sales.

## Strategies For Building High-Quality Backlinks

Several strategies can help you build high-quality backlinks for your website, including:

1.      Creating high-quality content: By creating high-quality and informative content, you can naturally attract backlinks from other websites that find your content useful.

2.      Guest blogging: Writing guest posts for other websites in your niche can help you gain exposure and backlinks to your website.

3.      Broken link building: This involves finding broken links on other websites and reaching out to the website owners to suggest replacing the broken link with a link to your content.

4.      Social media promotion: Sharing your content on social media platforms can increase its visibility and attract backlinks from other users.

5.      Influencer outreach: Reaching out to influencers and industry experts in your niche to collaborate on content can help you gain exposure and backlinks.

6.      Participating in online communities and forums: Being an active participant in online communities and forums related to your niche can help you build relationships with other website owners and gain backlinks.

# CHAPTER 7:
# TECHNICAL SEO

Technical SEO refers to the optimization of a website's technical elements to improve its search engine rankings and visibility. This involves making changes to a website's structure, code, and server configuration to make it easier for search engines to crawl and index the site's content.

Some common technical SEO practices include optimizing website speed and performance, improving website architecture and URL structure, implementing structured data markup, ensuring website security, and optimizing for mobile devices.

Website speed and performance are important factors in search engine rankings, as search engines prioritize fast-loading websites. Optimizing website architecture and URL structure can make it easier for search engines to crawl and index the site's content, which can improve its visibility in search results. Implementing structured data markup can help search engines understand the content on a website, which can result in rich snippets in search results.

Ensuring website security is important for both user experience and search engine rankings, as search engines prioritize secure websites. Optimizing for mobile devices is also important, as more and more users access the internet through mobile devices.

Technical SEO can be a complex process, and it's important to work with an experienced SEO professional or agency to ensure that your website is optimized for maximum visibility in search results.

Technical SEO refers to the optimization of your website's technical aspects to improve its visibility and search engine rankings. It involves ensuring that your website is accessible, functional, and easy for search engines to crawl and index.

Some key technical SEO considerations include:

Site speed: Slow-loading websites can negatively impact user experience and search engine rankings. Optimizing your website's code, compressing images, and reducing server response time can help improve your site speed.

Mobile optimization: With the majority of internet users accessing websites from mobile devices, it's essential to have a mobile-friendly website. This includes using responsive design, optimizing images and videos for mobile, and ensuring that your site's buttons and links are easy to tap on a small screen.

Site structure: Your site's structure should be organized and easy to navigate, both for users and search engines. This includes having a clear hierarchy of pages and using breadcrumb navigation, among other techniques.

URL structure: Your site's URLs should be clear and descriptive, making it easy for users and search engines to understand the content on each page. Avoid using long, complex URLs with lots of numbers or symbols.

HTTPS: Using HTTPS (HyperText Transfer Protocol Secure) instead of HTTP can help improve your site's security and can also give you a small SEO boost.

By optimizing these and other technical aspects of your website, you can help ensure that it is easily discoverable and accessible to both users and search engines.

## What Is Technical Seo?

Technical SEO refers to the process of optimizing a website's technical aspects to improve its search engine ranking and visibility. This involves making changes to the website's structure, code, and server configuration to make it easier for search engine crawlers to index and understand the content on the site.

Technical SEO covers a wide range of optimization techniques, including website speed and performance optimization, website architecture and URL structure optimization, mobile optimization, website security optimization, and structured data implementation.

By optimizing a website's technical aspects, it can improve its search engine ranking and visibility, resulting in increased traffic, engagement, and conversions. Technical SEO is a critical component of overall SEO strategy and should be done regularly to keep up with search engine algorithm updates and ensure that the website is up-to-date with current best practices.

Some common technical SEO tasks include optimizing website speed, improving website architecture, optimizing website images, ensuring website security, and implementing structured data markup. These tasks can be complex and require a certain level of technical expertise, so it's recommended to work with an experienced SEO professional or agency to ensure that the website is properly optimized.

# Importance Of Technical Seo

Technical SEO is important because it directly affects a website's search engine visibility and ranking. If a website is not optimized for technical SEO, it may not be easily crawled or indexed by search engines, which can result in a lower ranking and less visibility in search results.

Optimizing a website's technical aspects can improve website speed and performance, website architecture, and URL structure, mobile optimization, website security, and structured data implementation. All of these factors can contribute to a better user experience and increase the likelihood that users will engage with the website.

In addition, technical SEO can help ensure that search engines can effectively crawl and index the website's content, making it more likely that the website will rank well in search results for relevant keywords and phrases.

Overall, technical SEO is a critical component of any SEO strategy and should be regularly assessed and updated to keep up with changes to search engine algorithms and best practices. A well-optimized website can result in increased traffic, engagement, and conversions, ultimately leading to a better overall online presence and business success.

## Mobile Optimization

Mobile optimization refers to the process of optimizing a website for mobile devices, such as smartphones and tablets. With more and more people accessing the internet through mobile devices, mobile optimization is becoming increasingly important for website owners.

Mobile optimization involves several key factors, including responsive design, page speed, and mobile-friendly content. Some important considerations for mobile optimization include:

Responsive design: A responsive design allows a website to automatically adjust to different screen sizes and orientations, making it easy to use on both desktop and mobile devices.

Page speed: Mobile users are often on-the-go and may not have access to high-speed internet, so it's important to ensure that website pages load quickly on mobile devices.

Mobile-friendly content: Mobile users often have different browsing habits than desktop users, so it's important to provide content that is optimized for mobile devices. This can include shorter paragraphs, larger fonts, and simplified navigation.

Mobile-friendly forms: Forms on a website should be easy to fill out on a mobile device, with large input fields and clear instructions.

By optimizing a website for mobile devices, website owners can improve the user experience for mobile users and increase engagement and conversions. Additionally, search engines give preference to mobile-friendly websites in search results, so mobile optimization can also improve a website's search engine ranking.

## Mobile Responsiveness And Usability

Mobile responsiveness and usability are essential factors in technical SEO. With the increasing number of mobile users, search engines prioritize mobile-friendly websites in their search results. Therefore, it is crucial to ensure that your website is optimized for mobile devices, including smartphones and tablets.

Mobile responsiveness refers to the ability of a website to adjust its content and layout to fit various screen sizes and resolutions. A mobile-friendly website provides a seamless user experience, allowing visitors to access information quickly and easily on their mobile devices.

Usability, on the other hand, refers to the overall user experience of a website. It includes factors such as the site's navigation, layout, content, and functionality. A website that is easy to use and navigate enhances the user experience, which can lead to increased engagement and conversions.

To improve mobile responsiveness and usability, you can:

Use a responsive web design that automatically adjusts to fit different screen sizes and resolutions.

Optimize images and other media to reduce load times and improve page speed.

Use clear and concise headings, subheadings, and content that is easy to read on small screens.

Simplify your website's navigation and ensure that it is easy to use on mobile devices.

Use large, clickable buttons and links that are easy to tap with a finger.

Ensure that your website's forms and other interactive elements are optimized for mobile devices.

By optimizing your website for mobile responsiveness and usability, you can improve your search engine rankings, increase user engagement, and ultimately drive more conversions and revenue for your business.

## Page Speed And Load Times

Page speed and load times are crucial factors in technical SEO, as they can affect both user experience and search engine rankings. Site speed is a key factor in Google's algorithm, and faster-loading sites tend to rank higher in search engine results pages (SERPs) than slower-loading sites. In addition, users are more likely to stay on a site and engage with its content if it loads quickly, which can lead to higher conversions and increased revenue.

To improve page speed and load times, several best practices can be followed:

Minimize HTTP requests: This can be achieved by reducing the number of resources (images, scripts, etc.) that need to be downloaded by the browser.

Optimize images: Images are often the largest files on a web page, so optimizing them can have a big impact on load times. This can be done by compressing images, using the appropriate file format, and resizing images to the correct dimensions.

Use a content delivery network (CDN): A CDN can improve page speed by caching content on servers located closer to the user.

Enable browser caching: This allows the browser to store certain files (such as images and scripts) locally, which can speed up subsequent page loads.

Minimize HTML, CSS, and JavaScript: This can be achieved by removing unnecessary code and whitespace and combining and minifying files where possible.

Use a fast web host: The speed of the server hosting the website can also impact page speed and load times. Choosing a fast and reliable web host is important.

Implement lazy loading: This technique delays the loading of non-critical resources (such as images that are not immediately visible) until they are needed, which can improve page speed and load times.

## Schema Markup

Schema markup is a type of structured data that can be added to a website's HTML code to provide search engines with additional information about the content on the website. This structured data can help search engines better understand the meaning and context of the content on the website, which can lead to improved search engine results page (SERP) features, such as rich snippets, knowledge panels, and other enhanced search results.

Schema markup can be used to provide search engines with information about a variety of content types, including:

Products: Including information such as name, image, price, and availability.

Events: Including information such as date, time, location, and performers.

Recipes: Including information such as ingredients, cooking time, and nutrition information.

Local businesses: Including information such as an address, phone number, and business hours.

Articles: Including information such as headline, author, and publication date.

Schema markup can be implemented in many ways, including using JSON-LD, RDFa, or microdata. There are also several online tools available to help website owners and developers create and test schema markups on their websites.

Implementing schema markup on a website can help improve the visibility of the website in search results and increase click-through rates by providing users with more detailed and relevant information about the content on the website.

## Site Architecture

Site architecture refers to the way a website's pages and content are organized and structured. It includes factors such as the hierarchy of pages, the use of categories and tags, and the internal linking structure.

A well-organized site architecture can have many benefits, including:

Improved user experience: A clear and logical site architecture makes it easy for users to find the information they are looking for, which can increase engagement and reduce bounce rates.

Improved navigation: A well-organized site architecture makes it easy for users to navigate from one page to another, which can improve the overall flow of the website and increase engagement.

Improved search engine optimization (SEO): Search engines use site architecture to understand the content and structure of a website. A well-organized site architecture can improve a website's SEO by making it easier for search engines to crawl and index the website.

When designing a site architecture, it's important to consider factors such as the website's goals, the target audience, and the type of content being presented. Some best practices for site architecture include:

Using a logical hierarchy: Pages should be organized in a logical hierarchy, with important pages higher up in the hierarchy and less important pages deeper down.

Using categories and tags: Categories and tags can help organize content and make it easier for users to find what they are looking for.

Using internal linking: Internal linking can help guide users through the website and improve navigation, as well as help search engines understand the content and structure of the website.

Overall, a well-organized site architecture can have many benefits for both users and search engines, making it an important consideration for website owners and developers.

# Site Architecture And Navigation

Site architecture and navigation are crucial elements of technical SEO that affect website usability and search engine rankings. The way a website is structured and organized can impact how easily search engines crawl and index the content, and how users navigate and interact with the site.

Some best practices for site architecture and navigation include:

Clear and concise URL structure: URLs should be short, descriptive, and easy to read, with keywords that accurately reflect the content of the page.

Internal linking: Creating a logical internal linking structure can help search engines understand the hierarchy and organization of your content, and can also help users easily find related content on your site.

Mobile-friendliness: With more and more users accessing websites on mobile devices, it's essential to ensure that your site is optimized for mobile screens and that navigation is easy and intuitive on smaller screens.

Site speed: Fast loading times are important for both user experience and search engine rankings, so optimizing images and other media files, minimizing code and scripts, and using a content delivery network (CDN) can all help improve site speed.

Site maps: Creating a sitemap that lists all of your site's pages can help search engines easily crawl and index your content, and can also provide a useful reference for users looking to navigate the site.

By following these best practices, you can help ensure that your site is well-structured and easy to navigate, which can improve both user experience and search engine rankings.

## Site Speed

Site speed refers to the amount of time it takes for a website to load its content. It is an important factor in both user experience and search engine optimization. A slow-loading website can negatively impact user experience, as users are less likely to engage with a site that takes too long to load. Additionally, search engines take into account site speed when determining search engine rankings, with faster sites often being given priority over slower sites.

Several factors can affect site speed, including website design, hosting, image optimization, and website code. Some common ways to improve site speed include:

Optimizing website images: Images can be a major contributor to slow website loading times. Optimizing images by compressing their size without sacrificing quality can help speed up website loading times.

Minimizing website code: Reducing the amount of website code, such as HTML, CSS, and JavaScript, can help speed up website loading times.

Using a content delivery network (CDN): A CDN can help improve site speed by delivering content to users from a server that is closest to them.

Using caching: Caching can help reduce the amount of time it takes for a website to load by storing frequently accessed data in a temporary storage area.

Choosing a good hosting provider: A reliable hosting provider with fast server response times can help improve site speed.

Overall, optimizing site speed is an important factor in both user experience and search engine optimization. By improving site speed, websites can provide a better user experience and improve their search engine ranking, resulting in increased traffic and engagement.

# CHAPTER 8: CONTENT MARKETING

C ontent marketing refers to the process of creating and sharing valuable, relevant, and consistent content to attract and retain a clearly defined audience, ultimately driving profitable customer action. In the context of SEO, content marketing can be used to create high-quality content that helps to improve search engine rankings and attract more organic traffic to a website.

Content marketing involves researching and understanding the target audience, identifying their pain points and interests, and creating content that addresses those needs. This can include blog posts, articles, infographics, videos, social media posts, and more. The content should be optimized for both search engines and users, incorporating relevant keywords and providing value to the reader.

The goal of content marketing is not just to attract visitors to a website, but to build trust and credibility with the audience. By providing valuable information and insights, businesses can position themselves as thought leaders in their industry and establish a loyal following of customers and advocates.

Content marketing can also be used to support other SEO strategies, such as link-building and social media marketing. By creating high-quality content that is shareable and linkable, businesses can attract backlinks from other websites and generate social media buzz that can help to improve search engine rankings.

Content marketing is a digital marketing strategy that involves creating and sharing valuable, relevant, and consistent content to attract and retain a clearly defined audience. The goal of content marketing is to drive profitable customer action by providing helpful and informative content that addresses the needs and pain points of potential customers.

Content marketing is important for SEO because search engines like Google prioritize websites that provide high-quality, valuable, and relevant content. By creating content that is optimized for your target keywords and provides value to your audience, you can improve your website's search engine rankings and attract more organic traffic.

Types of content that perform well for SEO include blog posts, articles, infographics, videos, podcasts, and social media posts. To create effective content, it's important to research your target audience and their interests, as well as your industry and competitors. You should also optimize your content for your target keywords and use internal linking to connect related content on your website.

To promote your content, you can use social media, email marketing, and outreach to other websites and influencers in your industry. By creating and promoting high-quality content, you can improve your website's SEO and attract more traffic and leads to your business.

## What Is Content Marketing And Why It's Important For Seo

Content marketing is the practice of creating and distributing valuable, relevant, and consistent content to attract and retain a clearly defined audience to drive profitable customer action. It's important for SEO because search engines prioritize high-quality, relevant content that provides value to users.

By creating content that is optimized for search engines, businesses can increase their online visibility, drive traffic to their website, and ultimately generate leads and sales.

Content marketing also helps establish a business as a thought leader in its industry and can build trust and credibility with potential customers. Additionally, by creating shareable content, businesses can increase their reach and attract backlinks, which are an important factor in search engine rankings.

# Types Of Content That Perform Well For Seo

Many types of content perform well for SEO, including:

Blog posts: Regularly updated blog posts can help drive traffic to your website and establish your business as a thought leader in your industry.

Infographics: Infographics are highly shareable and can attract backlinks, making them a valuable asset for SEO.

Videos: Videos can improve engagement and time on site, which are important factors in search engine rankings.

How-to guides: How-to guides can provide value to users and establish your business as an authority in your industry.

Case studies: Case studies can demonstrate the effectiveness of your products or services and provide valuable insights for potential customers.

Whitepapers and research reports: Whitepapers and research reports can provide in-depth insights into your industry and establish your business as an expert in your field.

Ebooks: Ebooks can be used to generate leads and provide valuable information to potential customers.

Ultimately, the type of content that performs best for SEO will depend on your business and your target audience. It's important to conduct research and experiment with different types of content to determine what resonates with your audience and drives the most traffic and engagement.

## How To Create And Promote Content That Generates Traffic And Leads

To create and promote content that generates traffic and leads, you can follow these steps:

Identify your target audience and their needs: The first step is to identify your target audience and their needs. This will help you create content that is relevant and valuable to them.

Conduct keyword research: Use keyword research tools to identify the keywords and phrases that your target audience is using to search for information related to your business or industry.

Develop a content plan: Develop a content plan that includes a mix of different types of content, such as blog posts, videos, infographics, and social media updates. Make sure your plan is aligned with your business goals and is focused on addressing the needs of your target audience.

Create high-quality content: When creating content, focus on creating high-quality content that provides value to your audience. Use your target keywords and phrases strategically in your content, but don't overdo it or your content may come across as spammy.

Optimize your content for search engines: Make sure your content is optimized for search engines by including relevant keywords in your title, meta descriptions, and throughout the body of your content. Use header tags and bullet points to make your content easier to read and scan.

Promote your content: Promote your content through social media, email marketing, and other channels to reach a wider audience. Encourage your readers to share your content with their networks.

Measure and analyze your results: Use analytics tools to measure the performance of your content and identify areas for improvement. Use this data to refine your content strategy and optimize your content for better results.

## The Importance Of Content Marketing For Seo

Content marketing is crucial for SEO as it plays a significant role in driving traffic to your website, establishing your authority in your industry, and improving your search engine rankings.

Quality content attracts backlinks, shares, and engagement, all of which are signals to search engines that your website is authoritative and relevant to users.

Additionally, regularly publishing fresh, high-quality content can help search engines crawl and index your site more frequently, boosting your rankings.

Finally, content marketing also helps you target long-tail keywords, which are less competitive and can bring in highly targeted traffic to your website.

# Tips For Creating Engaging And Shareable Content

Sure, here are some tips for creating engaging and shareable content:

1.      Know your audience: Understanding your target audience is crucial for creating content that resonates with them. Research to determine what kind of content they are interested in and what type of language and tone will appeal to them.

2.      Create original content: Original content is more likely to be shared than content that has been copied from other sources. Make sure your content provides unique value to your audience.

3.      Use visuals: Including images, videos, and infographics can make your content more engaging and shareable. Visual content is often more memorable than text alone.

4.      Keep it concise: People are more likely to read and share content that is easy to digest. Make sure your content is concise and to the point.

5.      Use emotional triggers: People are more likely to share content that triggers an emotional response. Use storytelling and other techniques to create content that evokes emotions such as happiness, sadness, or anger.

6.      Use social media: Social media is a powerful tool for promoting and sharing content. Make sure your content is easily shareable on social media platforms by including social sharing buttons and crafting attention-grabbing headlines.

7.      Consistency: Consistency is key when it comes to content marketing. Develop a content calendar and stick to a regular publishing schedule. This will help you build an audience and keep them engaged with your brand.

# CHAPTER 9:
# COPYWRITING
# TECHNIQUES FOR SEO

Copywriting techniques for SEO involve creating high-quality, compelling content that is optimized for search engines and users. Here are some techniques to keep in mind:

Use relevant keywords: Use relevant keywords throughout the content, including in the title, headings, subheadings, and body. But be careful not to overuse keywords, as this can lead to keyword stuffing and negatively impact SEO.

Write compelling titles and meta descriptions: Titles and meta descriptions should accurately reflect the content of the page and include relevant keywords. They should also be written to entice users to click through to the page.

Use header tags: Use header tags (H1, H2, H3, etc.) to organize content and make it easier for search engines to understand the structure of the page.

Optimize images: Optimize images by using descriptive file

names and alt tags that include relevant keywords.

Write for the user: While it's important to include keywords, it's equally important to write for the user. Write content that is easy to read, engaging, and informative.

Use internal linking: Use internal linking to help users navigate to related content on the website and to help search engines understand the structure of the website.

Incorporate social media: Incorporate social media by adding social sharing buttons to the content to encourage users to share the content on social media.

By following these techniques, website owners can create high-quality, optimized content that is both search engine and user-friendly, leading to improved SEO performance and increased traffic, engagement, and conversions.

# Writing For Your Audience

Writing for your audience is an essential component of copywriting for SEO. While it's important to include relevant keywords and follow best practices for optimizing content for search engines, ultimately, the content should be written for the audience.

Here are some tips for writing for your audience:

Know your audience: Before you start writing, it's important to understand who your target audience is. This will help you create content that resonates with them and addresses their needs and interests.

Use language that your audience understands: Avoid using technical jargon or industry-specific terms that may not be familiar to your audience. Use language that is clear and easy to understand.

Address your audience's pain points: Identify the challenges or problems your audience is facing and address them in your content. This will help establish your authority and credibility and make your content more valuable to your audience.

Provide valuable information: Your content should provide valuable information that your audience can use. This could include how-to guides, tips, tricks, or other relevant information that helps your audience achieve their goals.

Use a conversational tone: Writing in a conversational tone can help make your content more engaging and relatable to your audience.

By writing for your audience, you can create content that is more relevant and valuable to them, which can lead to increased engagement, conversions, and loyalty.

## Crafting Compelling Headlines

Crafting compelling headlines is crucial for attracting readers and driving traffic to your website. Here are some tips to help you create effective headlines:

Keep it short and simple: Your headline should be concise and to the point. Use as few words as possible to convey your message.

Use strong adjectives: Using strong, descriptive adjectives can help make your headline more attention-grabbing. For example, instead of "How to Make Pancakes," try "Fluffy, Delicious Pancakes in Just 10 Minutes."

Use numbers: Including a number in your headline can make it more specific and compelling. For example, "10 Easy DIY Home Decor Ideas" is more effective than "Easy DIY Home Decor Ideas."

Address your audience's pain points: Use your headline to address a common problem or concern that your audience may have. For example, "5 Tips for Beating Procrastination and Getting More Done" targets a common pain point for many people.

Be unique and creative: Avoid using cliches or generic headlines. Try to come up with a unique angle or perspective that will make your content stand out.

Use keywords: Incorporate relevant keywords into your headlines to improve your search engine optimization (SEO) and help your content rank higher in search results.

Remember that your headline is often the first thing that readers will see, so it's important to make it as compelling and attention-grabbing as possible. By following these tips, you can create headlines that are more likely to attract readers and drive traffic to your website.

## Creating Engaging Content

Creating engaging content is key to keeping your audience interested and coming back for more. Here are some tips for creating content that is both informative and engaging:

Know your audience: Understanding your audience is crucial to creating content that resonates with them. Research your audience's interests, pain points, and demographics, and tailor your content to their needs.

Use storytelling: Incorporating storytelling elements into your content can help make it more engaging and memorable. Use anecdotes, examples, and personal experiences to help illustrate your points and connect with your audience.

Provide value: Your content should provide value to your audience, whether it's information, entertainment, or both. Make sure your content is informative, helpful, and relevant to your audience's interests and needs.

Use visuals: Incorporating images, videos, and other visual elements into your content can help break up long blocks of text and make your content more engaging. Use high-quality visuals that are relevant to your content.

Use a conversational tone: Writing in a conversational tone can help make your content more approachable and relatable to your audience. Avoid using overly technical or formal language that may be difficult for your audience to understand.

Incorporate calls to action: Encourage your audience to take action by including calls to action (CTAs) throughout your content. Whether it's signing up for a newsletter, following you on social media, or leaving a comment, CTAs can help increase engagement and build a loyal audience.

Remember that creating engaging content takes time and effort, but the rewards can be significant. By following these tips, you can create content that is both informative and engaging, and build a loyal audience that values your brand and content.

# Incorporating Keywords Naturally

Incorporating keywords into your content is important for SEO, but it's also important to do so naturally and organically so that doesn't feel forced or spammy. Here are some tips for incorporating keywords naturally:

Use long-tail keywords: Long-tail keywords are more specific phrases that are less competitive and easier to rank for. Using long-tail keywords can help you incorporate them naturally into your content.

Write for your audience first: Your content should always be written with your audience in mind, not search engines. Focus on providing valuable and engaging content that your audience will want to read, and then incorporate keywords where they make sense.

Use synonyms and related terms: Instead of using the same keyword over and over again, try using synonyms and related terms to make your content more varied and interesting. This can also help you rank for more related search terms.

Place keywords strategically: Place keywords in strategic locations, such as in the title tag, meta description, header tags, and throughout the body of the content. But don't overdo it - only use keywords where they make sense and flow naturally.

Use variations of your keywords: Use variations of your target keywords to keep your content fresh and interesting. This can also help you rank for related terms and avoid being penalized for keyword stuffing.

Edit and refine your content: After you've written your content, go back and review it to make sure your keywords are used naturally and in a way that makes sense. Edit and refine your content as needed to ensure it's engaging, informative, and optimized for SEO.

Remember, the most important thing is to focus on creating valuable and engaging content for your audience, rather than trying to stuff your content with keywords. By incorporating keywords naturally and organically, you can improve your SEO without sacrificing the quality of your content.

# Call To Action (Ctas)

Calls to action (CTAs) are an important part of any copywriting strategy, including SEO. A CTA is a phrase or statement that encourages a reader or website visitor to take a specific action, such as signing up for a newsletter, downloading a free guide, or making a purchase. Here are some tips for creating effective CTAs for your SEO-focused copy:

Be clear and specific: Your CTA should be clear and specific about what action you want the reader to take. Use active language, such as "Sign up now" or "Download our free guide".

Use urgency: Use language that creates a sense of urgency, such as "Limited time offer" or "Only a few spots left". This can help motivate readers to take action right away.

Place CTAs strategically: Place your CTAs in strategic locations throughout your content, such as at the end of blog posts or on landing pages. Make sure they stand out visually, using contrasting colors or bold text.

Make it easy to act: Make it as easy as possible for readers to take action by providing clear instructions and minimizing any barriers or obstacles. For example, if you want readers to sign up for a newsletter, keep the form short and simple.

Test and refine: Continuously test and refine your CTAs to see what works best for your audience. Try different languages, placements, and designs, and track your results to see which CTAs are most effective at driving conversions.

Remember, a well-crafted CTA can be a powerful tool for driving conversions and achieving your SEO goals. By following these tips and experimenting with different approaches, you can create CTAs that motivate readers to take action and improve your SEO performance.

# CHAPTER 10: ANALYTICS AND TRACKING

nalytics and Reporting

Analytics and reporting play a crucial role in any SEO campaign as they help you track and measure the success of your efforts. By analyzing data and metrics, you can gain insights into how your website is performing and make informed decisions about what changes to make to improve your SEO.

Some of the key metrics that you should be tracking include:

Traffic: This includes both the quantity and quality of traffic coming to your site.

Rankings: Keep an eye on your search engine rankings for your target keywords to see if your optimization efforts are paying off.

Conversions: Measure the number of visitors who take a desired action on your site, such as making a purchase, filling out a form, or downloading a resource.

Bounce rate: This metric measures the percentage of visitors who leave your site after viewing only one page.

Engagement metrics: Look at metrics such as time on site, pages per session, and social shares to gauge how engaged your visitors are with your content.

To track these metrics, you can use a variety of tools such as Google Analytics, which is a free analytics tool that allows you to track website traffic, user behavior, and other key metrics. You can also use other paid analytics tools that offer more advanced features and insights.

Reporting is also important because it helps you communicate the results of your SEO efforts to stakeholders such as clients, management, or other team members. Reporting can be done regularly, such as monthly or quarterly, and should include key metrics and insights, as well as recommendations for future improvements.

# Analytics And Tracking

Analytics and tracking are critical components of a successful online marketing campaign. By tracking website traffic and user behavior, businesses can gain valuable insights into their target audience and make data-driven decisions. Here are some key analytics and tracking strategies:

1. Set up website tracking: Use a web analytics tool, such as Google Analytics, to track website traffic and user behavior. Set up goals and events to track specific user actions, such as form submissions or product purchases.

2. Monitor key metrics: Keep track of key metrics, such as bounce rate, conversion rate, and average session duration. Use these metrics to identify areas for improvement and optimize the website accordingly.

3. Use A/B testing: Test different variations of landing pages, calls to action, and other website elements to see which performs better. Use A/B testing tools, such as Google Optimize, to set up and analyze tests.

4. Track social media engagement: Use social media analytics tools, such as Facebook Insights or Twitter Analytics, to track engagement and measure the effectiveness of social media campaigns.

5. Monitor email campaigns: Use email marketing analytics tools, such as Mailchimp or Constant Contact, to track open rates, click-through rates, and other metrics for email campaigns.

6. Use heat mapping: Use heat mapping tools, such as Crazy Egg or Hotjar, to visualize user behavior and identify areas of the website that need improvement.

7. Analyze customer feedback: Use tools like surveys or user testing to gather feedback from customers. Use

this feedback to improve the website and marketing campaigns.

By using analytics and tracking tools, businesses can gain valuable insights into their website performance and user behavior, which can help to optimize their online marketing efforts and improve the customer experience.

## Measuring Seo Success

Measuring the success of your SEO efforts is an important part of any SEO strategy. There are several metrics you can use to track and measure the success of your SEO efforts, including:

Organic search traffic: This measures the number of visitors to your website who arrived via organic search engine results. Increasing organic search traffic is a key goal of SEO.

Keyword rankings: Tracking the rankings of your target keywords can give you an idea of how well your content is performing on search engine results pages.

Conversion rate: This measures the percentage of website visitors who take a desired action, such as making a purchase or filling out a form. Improving your website's conversion rate is a key goal of SEO.

Backlink profile: The number and quality of backlinks pointing to your website can have a significant impact on your search engine rankings. Tracking your backlink profile and monitoring for changes can help you understand how your SEO efforts are impacting your website's authority and visibility.

Bounce rate: This measures the percentage of visitors who leave your website after viewing only one page. A high bounce rate can be an indicator of poor user experience, which can negatively impact your search engine rankings.

Page load time: This measures how long it takes for your website to load. Faster loading times can lead to improved user experience and better search engine rankings.

It's important to regularly track and analyze these metrics to understand how your SEO efforts are impacting your website's visibility, traffic, and conversions. By regularly monitoring and adjusting your SEO strategy based on these metrics, you can continue to improve the success of your SEO efforts over time.

## Key Performance Indicators

Key performance indicators (KPIs) are metrics that are used to measure the success of a specific business goal or objective. In the context of SEO, KPIs can be used to measure the effectiveness of your SEO efforts and track progress toward your SEO goals. Some common KPIs for SEO include:

Organic search traffic: This measures the number of visitors who arrive at your website through organic search engine results.

Keyword rankings: This measures how well your website and its pages rank in search engine results for specific keywords.

Conversion rate: This measures the percentage of visitors who complete a desired action on your website, such as filling out a form or making a purchase.

Bounce rate: This measures the percentage of visitors who leave your website after viewing only one page.

Backlinks: This measures the number and quality of external links pointing to your website, which can impact your search engine rankings.

Time on page: This measures how long visitors spend on a specific page on your website, which can indicate engagement with your content.

Page load time: This measures how long it takes for a page on your website to load, which can impact user experience and search engine rankings.

By setting specific, measurable KPIs and regularly tracking

progress towards these goals, you can better understand the effectiveness of your SEO efforts and make data-driven decisions to improve your website's visibility, traffic, and conversions.

## Google Analytics

Google Analytics is a web analytics service offered by Google that allows website owners and marketers to track and analyze website traffic. It provides insights into how visitors are interacting with a website, including information on where they are coming from, what pages they are viewing, how long they are staying on the site, and more.

Google Analytics can also be used to track specific goals or conversions, such as filling out a form, making a purchase, or signing up for a newsletter. This data can be used to better understand user behavior and optimize website performance.

To use Google Analytics, website owners need to install a tracking code on their website. This code collects data from visitors and sends it to the Google Analytics platform, where it is processed and presented in a user-friendly dashboard. Users can access a variety of reports, including audience demographics, behavior flow, and acquisition channels, to gain a deeper understanding of their website's performance.

Google Analytics is a powerful tool for optimizing website performance and improving user experience. By analyzing data on user behavior and engagement, website owners can make informed decisions about content, design, and marketing strategies to increase traffic, engagement, and conversions.

# How To Set Up And Use Google Analytics

Here are the steps to set up and use Google Analytics:

1. Create a Google Analytics account: Go to the Google Analytics website and sign in using your Google account credentials. If you don't have a Google account, create one.

2. Set up a property: Once you're signed in, click on the "Admin" button on the bottom left of the screen, then click "Create Property." Follow the prompts to set up a new property for your website.

3. Add the tracking code to your website: Once you have set up a property, you will need to add the Google Analytics tracking code to your website. Copy the tracking code from the Google Analytics website and paste it into the header section of your website's HTML code.

4. Verify tracking code installation: Once you've added the tracking code to your website, you can verify that it's working by using the Real-Time view in Google Analytics.

5. Set up goals and events: Goals and events allow you to track specific user actions on your website, such as form submissions or product purchases. Go to the "Admin" section, click on "Goals" or "Events," and follow the prompts to set up goals and events for your website.

6. View reports: Once you have set up your Google Analytics account, you can view reports on your website's traffic, user behavior, and more. Go to the "Reporting" section of Google Analytics to view reports on your website's performance.

Here are some tips for using Google Analytics effectively:

1. Set up custom reports: Use custom reports to track specific metrics and dimensions that are important to your business.

2. Use annotations: Annotations allow you to add notes to your Google Analytics reports to document changes to your website or marketing campaigns.

3. Set up alerts: Set up custom alerts to notify you when certain metrics or events occur on your website, such as a sudden increase in traffic or a drop in conversion rate.

4. Use Google Analytics with other tools: Use Google Analytics with other tools, such as Google Ads or Google Search Console, to get a more comprehensive view of your online performance.

By setting up and using Google Analytics, businesses can gain valuable insights into their website's performance and user behavior, which can help them make data-driven decisions to improve their online presence and achieve their marketing goals.

# Google Search Console

Google Search Console is a free web service offered by Google that allows website owners and webmasters to monitor and improve the performance of their websites in Google's search results. It provides insights into how Google crawls and indexes a website, as well as alerts for issues that may affect a website's visibility in search results.

Google Search Console provides a range of tools and reports, including:

Performance report: This report shows how often a website appears in Google's search results, which queries are used to find the website and the click-through rate for each query.

Coverage report: This report provides information on how many pages of a website are indexed by Google and highlights any indexing issues.

URL inspection tool: This tool allows webmasters to check how Google crawls and indexes specific pages on a website.

Sitemaps: Webmasters can submit sitemaps to Google Search Console to help Google better understand the structure of a website.

Security issues: Google Search Console alerts webmasters to any security issues on their website, such as malware or hacking attempts.

Mobile usability: This report highlights any issues with a website's mobile usability, which can impact its search rankings.

By using Google Search Console, website owners, and webmasters can better understand how Google crawls and indexes their websites, identify any issues that may impact visibility in search results, and optimize their websites for better performance.

# A/B Testing

A/B testing, also known as split testing, is a method of comparing two versions of a web page or app screen to determine which one performs better. The goal of A/B testing is to identify changes that can improve the performance of a website or app, such as increasing conversions or engagement.

A/B testing involves creating two versions of a web page or app screen that are identical except for one element, such as a headline, button color, or image. Half of the visitors or users are shown one version (A), while the other half are shown the second version (B). By comparing the performance metrics of the two versions, such as click-through rate or conversion rate, it is possible to determine which version performs better.

A/B testing can be used to test a wide range of elements on a website or app, such as:

Headlines and subheadings

Call-to-action buttons

Images and graphics

Navigation menus

Form fields and inputs

To conduct an A/B test, a testing platform or software is required. These tools allow a website or app owner to create multiple versions of a page or screen, divide traffic or users between them, and track performance metrics. Some popular A/B testing tools include Google Optimize, Optimizely, and VWO.

By using A/B testing, website, and app owners can continuously improve the user experience and increase engagement, ultimately leading to better performance and increased revenue.

# Monitoring And Improving Metrics

Monitoring and improving metrics is a crucial part of any SEO strategy. It involves tracking key performance indicators (KPIs) and using data-driven insights to make informed decisions about how to optimize a website or web page for search engines and users.

Here are some common metrics that can be used to monitor and improve SEO performance:

Organic traffic: This refers to the number of visitors to a website that comes from organic search engine results.

Keyword rankings: This refers to the position a website or web page ranks in search engine results for specific keywords.

Click-through rate (CTR): This refers to the percentage of clicks a website or web page receives in search engine results.

Bounce rate: This refers to the percentage of visitors who leave a website after only viewing one page.

Conversion rate: This refers to the percentage of website visitors who take a desired action, such as making a purchase or filling out a form.

To improve these metrics, website owners can make changes to their website or web page based on data-driven insights. For example, if the bounce rate is high, it may indicate that the website or web page is not meeting user expectations. Website owners can investigate why users are leaving the page and make changes to improve the user experience.

Similarly, if keyword rankings are low, website owners can investigate why their website or web page is not ranking well for those keywords and make changes to optimize for those keywords.

By monitoring and improving these metrics, website owners can continuously optimize their website or web pages for search engines and users, leading to improved SEO performance and increased traffic, engagement, and conversions.

# How To Track And Measure The Success Of Your Seo Efforts

To track and measure the success of your SEO efforts, you need to use analytics tools. There are many analytics tools available, but one of the most popular and widely used is Google Analytics.

Google Analytics is a free tool that provides valuable insights into your website's traffic and user behavior. It allows you to track a range of metrics, including the number of visitors to your site, how long they stay on your site, which pages they visit, and which pages they exit from.

To track your SEO efforts, you should focus on the following metrics:

Organic traffic: This refers to the number of visitors who find your site through search engines like Google.

Keyword rankings: This refers to where your site ranks in the search engine results pages (SERPs) for specific keywords.

Backlinks: This refers to the number and quality of links pointing to your site from other websites.

Conversion rate: This refers to the percentage of visitors who take a desired action on your site, such as making a purchase or filling out a contact form.

Once you have set up Google Analytics on your website, you can create custom reports to track these metrics over time. You can also use other tools, such as SEMrush or Ahrefs, to track your keyword rankings and backlinks.

By regularly tracking and analyzing these metrics, you can identify areas where you need to improve your SEO strategy and make data-driven decisions to optimize your website for better results.

## Key Metrics To Monitor, Such As Traffic, Rankings, And Engagement

Yes, monitoring key metrics is an important part of tracking and measuring the success of your SEO efforts. Some key metrics to monitor include:

Traffic: This includes the number of visitors to your website, as well as the sources of that traffic (e.g. organic search, social media, referrals, etc.)

Rankings: This refers to where your website and individual pages rank in search engine results pages (SERPs) for specific keywords.

Engagement: This includes metrics like time on site, bounce rate, and pages per session, which give you insight into how engaged visitors are with your website.

Conversions: This includes metrics like form fills, phone calls, and online purchases, which give you insight into how many website visitors are taking desired actions.

By monitoring these metrics, you can get a better understanding of how your SEO efforts are impacting your website's performance and make informed decisions about how to optimize your strategy moving forward.

# Key Metrics To Track For Seo And Conversion Optimization

Here are some key metrics to track for SEO and conversion optimization:

1.     Organic traffic: This is the number of visitors who find your website through organic search engine results. Tracking organic traffic over time can help you measure the effectiveness of your SEO efforts.

2.     Keyword rankings: Track the ranking positions of your target keywords to understand how well your SEO efforts are performing. Use a tool like Google Search Console or a third-party SEO tool to track your keyword rankings.

3.     Bounce rate: This metric measures the percentage of visitors who leave your website after viewing only one page. A high bounce rate can indicate issues with website usability or content quality.

4.     Conversion rate: This metric measures the percentage of website visitors who take a desired action, such as making a purchase or filling out a form. Tracking conversion rates over time can help you identify areas for improvement and optimize your website for better conversions.

5.     Average session duration: This metric measures the average amount of time visitors spend on your website. A longer average session duration can indicate higher engagement and interest in your website content.

6.     Exit rate: This metric measures the percentage of visitors who leave your website from a particular page. Tracking exit rates can help you identify pages that may need improvement or optimization.

7.     Click-through rate (CTR): This metric measures the percentage of users who click on a particular link or ad. CTR is commonly used to measure the effectiveness of paid search

campaigns.

8.      Cost per acquisition (CPA): This metric measures the cost of acquiring a new customer, such as the cost of running a paid search campaign. Tracking CPA can help you optimize your advertising spend and improve ROI.

By tracking these key metrics, businesses can gain valuable insights into their SEO and conversion optimization efforts, identify areas for improvement, and make data-driven decisions to improve their online marketing performance.

# The Importance Of Analytics In Seo And Copywriting

Analytics plays a critical role in both SEO and copywriting. Here's why:

1.	SEO: Analytics helps to track the performance of SEO efforts and make data-driven decisions to improve rankings and traffic. By tracking metrics such as organic traffic, keyword rankings, and backlinks, businesses can identify areas for improvement and optimize their SEO strategy accordingly. Analytics can also help to identify keyword opportunities, such as long-tail keywords or keywords with high search volume and low competition.

2.	Copywriting: Analytics helps to measure the effectiveness of copywriting efforts and make data-driven decisions to improve engagement and conversions. By tracking metrics such as bounce rate, time on page, and conversion rate, businesses can identify areas for improvement in their copywriting and optimize accordingly. Analytics can also help to identify which types of content are resonating with the target audience, such as blog posts or videos.

Overall, analytics is essential for both SEO and copywriting because it helps to measure performance, identify areas for improvement, and make data-driven decisions. By leveraging analytics, businesses can improve their online presence and achieve their marketing goals more effectively.

## How To Use Data To Inform Your Seo Strategy

Using data is crucial to inform and improve your SEO strategy. Here are some steps to follow:

Set up a tracking system: Use analytics tools like Google Analytics, SEMrush, Ahrefs, or other SEO tools to track and monitor your website's performance.

Define your goals: Identify your business objectives and SEO goals, such as increasing traffic, generating leads, or boosting conversions.

Analyze your data: Regularly review your data and analyze it to identify patterns, trends, and opportunities. Look at metrics like organic search traffic, bounce rate, time on site, and conversion rates.

Identify areas of improvement: Use your data to pinpoint areas where your SEO strategy needs improvement. For example, if you notice a high bounce rate on a particular page, it may indicate a problem with the content or user experience.

Optimize your strategy: Based on your analysis, refine and optimize your SEO strategy. This may involve tweaking your content, adjusting your targeting, or focusing on different keywords.

Monitor your progress: Continue to monitor your data and track your progress over time. This will allow you to see the impact of your optimizations and adjust your strategy as needed.

Overall, data-driven decision-making is key to achieving success with SEO. By regularly analyzing and optimizing your strategy based on your data, you can continuously improve your website's performance and drive more traffic and conversions.

# CHAPTER 11: CONVERSION OPTIMIZATION

SEO (Search Engine Optimization) and Conversion Optimization are two different strategies that can be used to improve the performance of a website, but they are not the same thing.

SEO is focused on optimizing a website's content and structure to rank higher in search engine results pages (SERPs). The goal of SEO is to increase the quantity and quality of organic traffic to a website. This involves various techniques such as keyword research, on-page optimization, link building, and technical SEO.

On the other hand, conversion optimization is focused on optimizing a website's user experience to increase the percentage of visitors who take a desired action, such as making a purchase, filling out a form, or subscribing to a newsletter. Conversion optimization involves analyzing user behavior, creating compelling content and calls to action, improving website usability, and testing different variations of website elements.

While both SEO and conversion optimization is important for a successful online business, they serve different purposes. SEO drives traffic to a website, while conversion optimization helps to convert that traffic into customers. A well-optimized website should focus on both SEO and conversion optimization to achieve the best results.

## Understanding The Conversion Funnel

The conversion funnel is a model that describes the stages that a potential customer goes through on their way to making a purchase or taking a desired action on a website. It is called a funnel because the number of potential customers decreases as they move through the stages, similar to how the number of liquid particles decreases as they move through a funnel.

The conversion funnel typically consists of four stages:

1. Awareness: At this stage, the potential customer becomes aware of a product or service. They may have seen an advertisement, heard about it from a friend, or stumbled upon it while browsing the internet. The goal at this stage is to attract the attention of potential customers and get them interested in the product or service.

2. Interest: At this stage, the potential customer is interested in the product or service and wants to learn more. They may visit the website, read product descriptions, and compare prices. The goal at this stage is to provide information and build trust with the potential customer.

3. Decision: At this stage, the potential customer is ready to make a decision and is considering whether to make a purchase or take a desired action. They may add the product to their cart, fill out a form, or sign up for a trial. The goal at this stage is to make it easy for the customer to complete the desired action and overcome any objections they may have.

4. Action: At this final stage, the potential customer takes the desired action, such as making a purchase, subscribing to a service, or filling out a form. The goal at this stage is to make the process as smooth as

possible and provide a positive customer experience.

By understanding the conversion funnel, businesses can optimize their website and marketing efforts to guide potential customers through each stage and increase the likelihood of them taking the desired action.

## Strategies For Optimizing Landing Pages And Calls To Action

Landing pages and calls to action are critical components of a successful online marketing campaign. They are the first things a potential customer sees when they visit a website, and they can have a significant impact on whether the customer takes the desired action, such as making a purchase or filling out a form. Here are some strategies for optimizing landing pages and calls to action:

1. Keep it simple: A landing page should have a clear and simple message that is easy to understand. Use concise and straightforward language to convey the benefits of the product or service.

2. Highlight the value proposition: Clearly state what makes your product or service unique and how it will benefit the customer. Use bullet points, images, or videos to showcase the features and benefits of the product.

3. Make the call to action prominent: The call to action should be clearly visible and prominently displayed on the landing page. Use contrasting colors and white space to draw attention to the call to action button.

4. Use persuasive language: Use action-oriented language and strong verbs to encourage the customer to take action. For example, instead of "Submit," use "Get started today" or "Sign up now."

5. Test different variations: Test different variations of the landing page and call to action to see which performs better. Experiment with different colors, text, and placement of the call to action button to find the best combination.

6. Provide social proof: Use customer testimonials,

reviews, and ratings to build trust and credibility with potential customers. Social proof can help to overcome objections and encourage the customer to take action.

7. Optimize for mobile devices: Ensure that the landing page is optimized for mobile devices, with a responsive design that adapts to different screen sizes. Mobile optimization is crucial as more and more people are browsing the internet on their smartphones.

By following these strategies, businesses can optimize their landing pages and call to action to improve the chances of converting potential customers into paying customers.

# CHAPTER 12: STAYING UP-TO-DATE WITH SEO TRENDS

S taying up-to-date with SEO trends is important to ensure that your website stays optimized and competitive in search engine rankings. Here are some tips for staying up-to-date with SEO trends:

1. Follow SEO experts and influencers: Follow industry leaders and experts in SEO on social media platforms like Twitter, LinkedIn, and Facebook to stay informed about the latest trends and developments in SEO.

2. Attend conferences and events: Attend SEO conferences and events to learn about new techniques and strategies in the industry, and to network with other SEO professionals.

3. Read industry publications and blogs: Subscribe to industry publications and blogs to stay informed about the latest trends and best practices in SEO.

4. Participate in online communities: Join online communities like Reddit, Quora, and online forums to discuss SEO-related topics and stay informed about the latest trends and news.

5. Keep an eye on search engine updates: Regularly check for updates from search engines like Google, Bing, and Yahoo to stay informed about changes to their algorithms and ranking factors.

6. Use SEO tools and software: Use SEO tools and software like Google Analytics, SEMrush, Ahrefs, and Moz to analyze your website's performance, track your rankings, and identify areas for improvement.

7. Experiment and test: Keep testing new SEO techniques and strategies on your website to see what works best for your specific audience and industry.

By staying up-to-date with SEO trends, businesses can stay competitive and improve their search engine rankings, which can lead to increased website traffic and more conversions.

## The Ever-Changing Landscape Of Seo

The landscape of SEO is constantly changing, with search engines like Google regularly updating their algorithms and ranking factors to provide users with the best possible search results. Here are some reasons why the SEO landscape is constantly changing:

1. Advancements in technology: As technology evolves, search engines need to adapt to provide users with the most relevant and up-to-date information. For example, the rise of mobile devices has led to a greater focus on mobile-friendly websites and voice search optimization.

2. Changes in user behavior: As user behavior changes, search engines need to adjust their algorithms to provide the best possible search results. For example, the increasing popularity of visual search has led to the development of new image recognition technologies.

3. Competition: As more businesses compete for top search engine rankings, search engines need to update their algorithms to ensure that the most relevant and high-quality websites are ranked at the top of search results.

4. Black hat SEO techniques: The use of black hat SEO techniques, such as keyword stuffing and link spamming, can manipulate search engine rankings and undermine the integrity of search results. To combat these techniques, search engines regularly update their algorithms to penalize websites that engage in such practices.

To stay ahead in the ever-changing landscape of SEO, businesses need to remain agile and adaptable, and continually update their SEO strategies and techniques to meet the evolving needs of search engines and users. By staying informed about the latest SEO trends and best practices, businesses can optimize their websites for maximum search engine visibility and improve their online marketing performance.

## Strategies For Staying Up-To-Date With The Latest Seo Trends And Best Practices

Staying up-to-date with the latest SEO trends and best practices is essential to maintaining a successful online marketing strategy. Here are some strategies for staying up-to-date with the latest SEO trends:

1. Follow industry experts: Follow SEO experts on social media platforms like Twitter, LinkedIn, and Facebook. Subscribe to their blogs and podcasts, and attend webinars they host to stay updated on the latest SEO trends and best practices.

2. Attend SEO conferences and events: Attend industry conferences and events to learn about the latest SEO strategies and techniques. These events often feature presentations from leading SEO experts and provide opportunities to network with other professionals in the industry.

3. Join SEO communities: Join online communities like Reddit, Quora, and online forums to discuss SEO-related topics with peers and learn about the latest trends and news.

4. Read industry publications: Subscribe to industry publications and blogs to stay informed about the latest SEO trends and best practices.

5. Utilize SEO tools: Use SEO tools like SEMrush, Ahrefs, and Moz to stay up-to-date with the latest SEO trends, analyze your website's performance and identify areas for improvement.

6. Experiment and test: Experiment with new SEO techniques and strategies to see what works best for your website and audience. Test different strategies and track their impact on your website's search engine

rankings and traffic.

7. Stay informed about search engine updates: Keep an eye on updates from search engines like Google, Bing, and Yahoo to stay informed about changes to their algorithms and ranking factors.

By staying up-to-date with the latest SEO trends and best practices, businesses can optimize their websites for maximum search engine visibility, improve their online marketing performance, and stay ahead of the competition.

# CONCLUSION

In conclusion, SEO is a critical component of any digital marketing strategy, and effective copywriting is essential for optimizing your website for search engines and converting visitors into customers.

By understanding the importance of keywords, on-page optimization, off-page optimization, technical SEO, content marketing, and analytics and reporting, you can create and implement an effective SEO strategy that drives traffic, generates leads, and grows your business.

Keep in mind that SEO is an ongoing process, and it requires continual analysis and refinement to stay ahead of the competition and maintain your search engine rankings. With the right tools, techniques, and strategies, however, you can achieve long-term success and reach your online marketing goals.

SEO is a critical component of online marketing and plays a significant role in driving traffic to websites and increasing conversions. Implementing effective SEO strategies can be challenging, as the landscape of SEO is constantly changing, with search engines regularly updating their algorithms and ranking factors to improve search results for users.

However, by staying up-to-date with the latest SEO trends

and best practices, businesses can optimize their websites for maximum search engine visibility and improve their online marketing performance. This can lead to increased website traffic, higher search engine rankings, and more conversions, ultimately helping businesses to achieve their marketing goals and grow their online presence.

In conclusion, SEO is an important aspect of any digital marketing strategy, and copywriting is a crucial component of successful SEO. By conducting thorough keyword research, optimizing on-page and off-page elements, and continually monitoring and refining your SEO performance, you can improve your search engine rankings and drive more traffic to your website.

Effective copywriting techniques, such as writing for your audience, crafting compelling headlines, creating engaging content, incorporating keywords naturally, and using effective CTAs, can also help you achieve your SEO goals. With the right approach and ongoing effort, you can create copy that not only appeals to your target audience but also helps you achieve your SEO objectives.

## Tips For Ongoing Seo Success

Here are some tips for ongoing SEO success:

Stay up to date with SEO trends and algorithm changes. The world of SEO is constantly evolving, and staying informed can help you stay ahead of the curve.

Regularly review and update your content to ensure it remains relevant and valuable to your audience.

Continue to build high-quality backlinks to your site, focusing on earning links from reputable and relevant sources.

Monitor your analytics regularly to track your progress and identify areas for improvement.

Stay active on social media and other relevant online communities to build your brand and attract new visitors to your site.

Consider investing in paid advertising or other marketing tactics to supplement your SEO efforts.

Continually test and refine your SEO strategy to ensure you're maximizing your results and achieving your goals.

# A Recap Of Key Takeaways

Sure! Here's a recap of some key takeaways from the book "SEO Best Practices for Beginners in Copywriting to Generate Traffic to Your Business Website and Convert Visitors into Customers":

SEO is an essential component of any successful digital marketing strategy. It helps you rank higher in search engine results, drive traffic to your site, and ultimately increase conversions.

Keyword research is the foundation of effective SEO. Use tools like Google Keyword Planner and SEMrush to find and choose the right keywords for your business.

On-page optimization involves optimizing page titles, meta descriptions, header tags, and other elements of your website to make it more search-engine friendly.

Backlinks are an important ranking factor in SEO. Focus on building high-quality backlinks from reputable websites to boost your site's authority.

Content marketing is a powerful way to generate traffic and leads. Types of content that perform well for SEO include blog posts, infographics, and videos.

Analytics and reporting are essential for tracking the success of your SEO efforts. Use tools like Google Analytics to monitor key metrics such as traffic, rankings, and engagement.

By implementing these key takeaways, businesses can create a successful SEO strategy that drives traffic to their website, increases conversion rates, and helps them achieve their marketing goals.

# Best Practices For Improving Website Usability And User Experience

Improving website usability and user experience (UX) is critical to the success of any online business. Here are some best practices for improving website usability and UX:

1. Simplify navigation: Ensure that the website navigation is easy to use and understand. Use clear and concise labels for navigation links and organize them logically.

2. Optimize page speed: Improve the website's loading speed to reduce the bounce rate and improve user experience. Use tools like Google's PageSpeed Insights to identify and fix performance issues.

3. Make it mobile-friendly: Ensure that the website is optimized for mobile devices with a responsive design that adapts to different screen sizes. Test the website on different devices to ensure that it is easy to use and navigate.

4. Use clear and concise content: Use simple language and clear headings to make it easy for users to understand the content. Use bullet points, images, and videos to break up long blocks of text.

5. Ensure accessibility: Make sure the website is accessible to people with disabilities. Use alt tags for images, provide text descriptions for audio and video content, and ensure that the website can be navigated using a keyboard.

6. Use white space effectively: Use white space to make the website more visually appealing and improve readability. White space can also help to guide the user's eye to important elements on the page.

7. Make it easy to contact: Provide clear and easy-to-

find contact information, such as phone numbers and email addresses. Use a contact form to make it easy for users to reach out and ask questions.

8. Test and iterate: Continuously test the website and make improvements based on user feedback. Use tools like Google Analytics and user testing to gather data and insights on user behavior.

By following these best practices, businesses can improve the usability and user experience of their website, which can lead to increased engagement, higher conversion rates, and ultimately, more satisfied customers.

# Future Of Seo In Copywriting

As technology and user behavior continue to evolve, the future of SEO in copywriting will likely see some changes and advancements. Here are some trends and predictions for the future of SEO in copywriting:

Voice search optimization: With the growing use of virtual assistants like Siri and Alexa, optimizing content for voice search will become increasingly important. This will involve targeting long-tail keywords and using more conversational language in your content.

Artificial intelligence (AI): AI technology is already being used in SEO to analyze data and provide insights for optimizing content. In the future, AI could be used to generate more personalized content based on user data and behavior.

User experience (UX) optimization: Google has been emphasizing the importance of user experience in search rankings, and this trend is expected to continue. Copywriters will need to focus on creating content that not only satisfies search algorithms but also provides value and a positive user experience.

Video content: Video content is becoming increasingly popular, and search engines are starting to incorporate video results into search rankings. Copywriters will need to create more video content and optimize it for search.

Local SEO: As more people use mobile devices to search for local businesses, optimizing for local search will become increasingly important. This will involve targeting location-based keywords and optimizing content for local search directories.

Overall, the future of SEO in copywriting will likely involve a continued focus on providing high-quality content that satisfies both search algorithms and user intent. As technology and user behavior continue to evolve, copywriters will need to stay up-to-date on the latest trends and adapt their strategies accordingly.

# Future Trends And Developments In Seo

In general, the field of SEO is constantly evolving, and we will likely continue to see advancements and changes in the future. Some potential trends and developments in SEO may include:

Voice search optimization: With the rise of smart speakers and voice assistants, optimizing for voice search may become increasingly important in the future.

Artificial intelligence and machine learning: These technologies may play a larger role in SEO, helping to analyze and optimize content, as well as make predictions about search patterns and behaviors.

Personalization: As search engines become more sophisticated, they may begin to personalize search results based on individual user preferences and behaviors.

User experience: Search engines are placing a greater emphasis on user experience, so optimizing for factors such as page speed, mobile responsiveness, and usability will continue to be important.

Featured snippets: These are short snippets of content that appear at the top of search results, and optimizing for them may become more important in the future.

Overall, it's important to stay up-to-date with the latest trends and developments in SEO to ensure that your website remains optimized for search engines and continues to generate traffic and leads.

# Final Thoughts And Recommendations

In today's digital age, SEO is a crucial component of any successful content marketing strategy. Copywriters need to understand how to optimize their content for search engines while still creating high-quality, engaging content that resonates with their audience.

To achieve this, it's important to conduct thorough keyword research, understand on-page and off-page SEO techniques, and use analytics tools to measure and improve performance. It's also crucial to stay up-to-date on the latest SEO trends and technologies to ensure that your content remains relevant and effective.

In addition, always remember to focus on your audience and create content that speaks to their needs and interests. Use compelling headlines and CTAs to grab their attention and encourage them to engage with your content. And don't forget to monitor and measure your performance regularly to ensure that your SEO strategy is working effectively.

Overall, SEO is a constantly evolving field, and copywriters need to stay informed and adapt their strategies accordingly. By prioritizing high-quality content and staying up-to-date on the latest trends and technologies, you can create content that resonates with your audience and drives traffic to your website.

# Final Thoughts On Seo And Copywriting For Business Websites

SEO and copywriting are two crucial components of creating a successful online presence for any business website. By optimizing your website for search engines and creating high-quality, engaging content, you can attract more traffic to your website and increase conversions.

It's essential to understand the best practices and trends in SEO and copywriting and stay up-to-date with the latest techniques to ensure your website stays ahead of the competition. Implementing effective SEO strategies and creating compelling copy requires a combination of technical knowledge, creativity, and data analysis.

Ultimately, the goal of SEO and copywriting is to create a seamless user experience that guides visitors through the conversion funnel and inspires them to take action. By focusing on the needs and interests of your target audience, and continually testing and refining your strategies, you can create a successful online marketing strategy that drives traffic, increases conversions, and helps you achieve your business goals.

# AFTERWORD

Congratulations, you've made it to the end of "SEO Best Practices For Beginners: In Copywriting To Generate Traffic To Your Business Website And Convert Visitors Into Customers"! By now, you should have a solid understanding of the fundamental principles of SEO and copywriting and how they work together to drive more traffic to your website and convert visitors into customers.

Remember, SEO is an ongoing process that requires constant monitoring, analysis, and optimization. The techniques and strategies covered in this book are just the beginning, and there is always more to learn and explore. Keep up with the latest SEO trends, tools, and techniques, and continue to experiment and refine your approach over time.

I hope this book has provided you with practical, actionable advice that you can use to improve your website's online visibility and drive more conversions. I also hope it has sparked your curiosity and inspired you to continue learning and exploring the exciting world of SEO and digital marketing.

Thank you for reading "SEO Best Practices For Beginners: In Copywriting To Generate Traffic To Your Business Website And Convert Visitors Into Customers". If you have any questions or feedback, please don't hesitate to reach out. I wish you all the best in your SEO and digital marketing endeavors!

# ACKNOWLEDGEMENT

I would like to express my sincere thanks to everyone who contributed to the creation of this book.

First and foremost, I want to thank my family and friends for their unwavering support and encouragement throughout the writing process. Their love and support kept me going when the going got tough.

I would also like to thank my colleagues and clients in the digital marketing industry who have shared their expertise and insights with me over the years. Their guidance and feedback have been invaluable in shaping my approach to SEO and copywriting.

Special thanks go out to my editor, who worked tirelessly to polish and refine this book and make it the best it could be. Their attention to detail and commitment to quality have been instrumental in bringing this project to fruition.

Finally, I want to thank you, the reader, for choosing "SEO Best Practices For Beginners: In Copywriting To Generate Traffic To Your Business Website And Convert Visitors Into Customers". I hope this book has provided you with practical, actionable advice that you can use to improve your website's online visibility and drive more conversions. Your interest and support mean the world to me.

Thank you all for being a part of this journey.

# ABOUT THE AUTHOR

## Ali Muattar

Ali Muattar is a digital marketer and SEO expert with over 20 years of experience in the field. He has helped businesses of all sizes improve their online visibility and drive more traffic to their websites through strategic SEO and content marketing initiatives.

Ali Muattar has a Bachelor's degree in Psychology with Mass Communication and a Master's degree in Psychology from the University of Karachi. He is a tech-based serial entrepreneur and seasoned professional, helping businesses across the globe.

In addition to his work in digital marketing, Ali Muattar is also a seasoned copywriter with a passion for creating engaging and persuasive content that resonates with readers. He has written for a variety of industries, including healthcare, finance, technology, and e-commerce.

When he's not working on SEO and content marketing campaigns, Ali Muattar enjoys reading about the latest developments in digital marketing, hiking, and spending time with his family and pets.

Ali Muattar's expertise and passion for digital marketing and copywriting are evident throughout this book. He has distilled years of experience and knowledge into practical, actionable advice that will help readers of all levels improve their website's SEO and drive more conversions.

# ANISH SEO BOOK SERIES

The "ANish SEO Book Series" is a comprehensive collection of books designed to help businesses and digital marketers improve their online visibility and drive more traffic to their websites through effective search engine optimization (SEO) techniques.

In "SEO Best Practices For Beginners: In Copywriting To Generate Traffic To Your Business Website And Convert Visitors Into Customers", readers will learn the fundamental principles of SEO and copywriting and how to use them to attract more visitors to their websites and turn them into customers. This book covers everything from keyword research and on-page optimization techniques to link-building and social media marketing.

Each book in the series is written by a seasoned digital marketing professional with years of experience in the field. The authors share their expertise and insights into the latest SEO trends, tools, and techniques, providing readers with practical, actionable advice they can use to improve their website's online visibility and drive more conversions.

Whether you're a small business owner looking to improve your website's SEO and copywriting or a digital marketer seeking to enhance your skills, the "ANish SEO Book Series" has something for everyone. Each book is easy to understand and filled with real-world examples and practical tips that readers can start implementing right away.

If you're serious about succeeding in the digital marketplace, the "SEO Book Series" is an essential resource that will help you achieve your goals and drive more traffic to your website.

## The Beginner's Guide To Seo Copywriting: Boosting Your Website's Traffic And Conversions

## Seo Writing 101: A Step-By-Step Guide To Writing For Search Engines

## Copywriting For Seo: How To Write Content That Ranks And Converts

## The Ultimate Guide To Seo Copywriting For Beginners

## Seo Copywriting Mastery: Proven Techniques To Drive Traffic And Boost Sales

## Seo Copywriting Made Easy: A Beginner's Guide To Writing For Search Engines

## The Power Of Words: Seo Copywriting Strategies To Transform Your Business

## Seo Copywriting For E-Commerce: Strategies For Driving Traffic And Conversions

From Keywords To Customers: The Ultimate Guide To Seo Copywriting

The Anatomy Of Seo Copywriting: Writing Content That Ranks And Converts

Seo Copywriting Secrets: Tips And Tricks For Boosting Traffic And Sales

Seo Writing For Beginners: The Ultimate Guide To Getting Your Content Found

Copywriting And Seo: How To Write Content That Gets Results

Seo Copywriting Strategies: The Beginner's Guide To Writing For Search Engines

Boosting Your Business With Seo Copywriting: A Step-By-Step Guide For Beginners

Seo Copywriting Hacks: The Ultimate Guide To Writing For Search Engines

Copywriting For The Web: How To Write Content

**That Gets You Noticed**

**Seo Copywriting Fundamentals: The Essential Guide For Beginners**

**The Art Of Seo Copywriting: How To Create Content That Sells**

**Seo Copywriting Wizardry: Advanced Techniques For Boosting Traffic And Conversions**